DELIVERANCE FROM DEMONS

THE CONFLICT BETWEEN GOD AND SATAN
BOOK 2

ZACHARIAS TANEE FOMUM

Copyright © 1985 by Zacharias Tanee Fomum
All rights reserved.

No part of this book may be reproduced in any form or by any electronic or mechanical means, including information storage and retrieval systems, without written permission from the author, except for the use of brief quotations in a book review.

Unless stated otherwise, the version of the Bible used in this book is the Revised Standard Version.

Published by

books4revival.com

A division of the Book Ministry of Christian Missionary Fellowship International

info@books4revival.com

I dedicate this book to

Patience NGOZI IFEADIKE

in loving and profound gratitude for her prayer, support and sacrifice in many ways, without which this book might never have been written.

CONTENTS

Preface	vii
1. Demons!	1
2. The Attack of Believers by Demons	23
3. The Ministry of Jesus to Demon - Attacked People	61
4. The Ministry of Believers to Demon-Attacked People	81
5. Keeping Free From Demons or Terminating With The Past	99
Back Matter	119

PREFACE

When the lord first laid it on my heart to teach the church in Yaounde, of which I am one of the teaching elders, on "Deliverance from Demons and Evil spirits", As usual, I took time to read the new Testament over and over in order to see afresh what it said about the subject. After all the preparation was over, I sat down in my office in our *"Clinic for Spiritual Diseases"*, to write the talks. It was then that I found out that I was in for big trouble. First of all, the light in the office began to go on and off in an unprecedented way. I could not work normally. On same evenings, I would get paralysed in my right hand and not be able to write, but when I stood up to go home, I would be instantly healed. One night, I felt too sick in my heart, head, body and all, that I went home feeling that was my last night on earth. Because of these attacks, I made little progress with the book. It was then that one of my co-labourer in the Lord, offered to pray for me as I wrote. So while I wrote, she prayed. I was then able to finish those talks and deliver them. Because of those messages, the

PREFACE

deliverance ministry was restored to many assemblies in the country and we thank GOD for it.

The devil did not sit quiet while his captives were released. The message received attacks from some believers, who without having cast out a single demon from an unbeliever, thought they knew what and how the deliverance ministry should be. Such attacks are expected for this book.

It is now nearly four years since those messages were written and preached. The burden has remained on me to see competent believers deliver those who are attacked by demons. The increase in the number of people needing deliverance in our ministry and the havoc being done on the Kingdom by demons, compelled me to write out those original talks into this book.

I have done under severe attacks from the enemy. I will not share what has been done by the prince of demons to stop me from writing this book. Suffice it to say that the fight has been fierce very fierce.

Now the book has been written and will be produced. I thank the Lord Jesus, the victorious king, who disarmed principalities and powers, and made a public show of them, triumphing over them on his cross and who is my Lord and helper. I thank all the saints who fasted and prayed for me while I was writing this book. I cannot imagine what is would have been like without them.

I send this book out with prayer that the Lord will use it to bless you and to bless others through you. May the Lord use it to make a contribution to the destruction of the ill-fated kingdom of Satan

PREFACE

I have read extensively on the subject. I am most grateful for help received from the book, *"War on the Saints"* by Jesie Pen Lewis and *Deliver us from Evil* By Don Basham.

Douala, 24th March 1985.

Zacharias TANEE FOMUM
B.P. 6090 YAOUNDE?
CAMEROON
WEST AFRICA.

1
DEMONS!

INTRODUCTION

God set out in the beginning to establish His Kingdom. The devil rebelled and decided to establish I rival kingdom The purpose of the devil is to imitate the kingdom of God, fight against it and if possible, overthrow it. The kingdom of God. Satan was once a mighty prince of God. He has full knowledge of the set up in the kingdom of God. Whenever we encounter a manifestation of Satanic power, we can be sure that there is a divine power in existence of which that satanic manifestation is an imitation. Let us look at some examples. There is a satanic trinity even as there is the holy trinity.

THE HOLY SPIRIT —> **The flesh**
THE LORD JESUS —> **The devil**
THE FATHER —> **The world.**

The satanic trinity is headed by the devil. The HOLY Trinity is headed by God the Father. The satanic trinity and kingdom is the masterpiece of Satan. The Holy Trinity and kingdom is the masterpiece of God.

The devil's kingdom is the kingdom of this world. He is the prince and ruler of heaven. God intended that man should, in co-operation with him, rule and dominate the earth. The devil stepped in deceived man and led him astray, and is using him on earth to oppose God.

Man is the centre of the conflict between God and Satan. The purpose of God is that man should be totally his and that his will should be wholly his and that his will should be done in all the earth. Because of these two masters, who are 100% opposed to each other, there is conflict.

This conflict means that there is no neutral position. Neutrality is absolutely impossible :

- You either have God for your father or the devil is your father
- Each of your thoughts works either for God or for the devil.
- Each of your worlds either works for God or for the devil.
- Each of your actions either works for God or for the devil.

There are no neutral thoughts, worlds or action. There are no innocent thoughts, words, or action Each one is a part of the warfare:

It is ultimately not a matter of good or bad thoughts, words or actions.

DEMONS!

It is ultimately not a matter of a useful thought world or action.

It is a matter of whether is serves God or it serves the devil.

It is a matter of its ultimate use.

Some things may be apparently useful in the service of God, for example, a little compromise here and there may appear to serve the interest of God in the immediate present but they will be seen in the final analyses to have been instrumental in building the devil's kingdom

When faced with a choice, do not ask whether it is good or bad; whether it is useful or useful or useless. The real question is whether it is of God or of Satan. The question is not whether this action will serve the interest of God now we are not living for now. The question is whether this action will serve the interest of God:

- now and
- tomorrow and
- next year and
- in a thousand year, and
- when viewed by God from the stand point of eternity.

Those who are to co-operate with God in the building of his kingdom and in the overthrow of that of satan, must do everything, not just for the moment, but with eternity in view. This is important. All action must also be viewed from two perspectives:

1. Its contribution in the building up of the kingdom of God.

2. Its contribution in the breaking down and the overthrow of the kingdom of Satan.

It is not enough that a person be involved in the building up of the kingdom of God. He must also be involved in the breaking down of the kingdom of Satan.

A man of spiritual consequence must be known in the kingdom of God where he bring joy by his contribution in building it he must also be known in the kingdom of darkness where he brings sorrow by his contribution in destroying it. There is a sense in witch some of the favourites in heaven do not carry out any building action. They just concentrate on the destruction of the kingdom of darkness.

Because of the gravity of the conflict, the enemy's army is well arranged and well ordered. In addition to the satanic trinity, there is the following line up:

1. Principalities,
2. Powers,
3. World rulers of this present darkness,
4. Spiritual hosts of wickedness in heavenly places,
5. Demons,

The five groups are five orders. There are a number of principalities possibly arranged in order of importance. Hierarchy is of immediate superior is of primary importance. Orders are given by Satan and they flow down to the one who is to discharge them, through his immediate superior. The devil does not leave it to his army to decide how they are to act. Things are imposed upon each one. There is no room in the Satanic kingdom for people wanting personal glory. There is one person who must receive all the glory and only one - Satan. Oh! That believers would forget their personal glorious kingdoms and interests and work for he glory of Jesus and only for His glory alone.

EVIL SPIRITS

Principalities, powers, world rules of this present darkness, spiritual hosts of wickedness in heavenly places and demons are all evil spirits. They are evil spirit for twos.

First of all, they are all spirits.

Secondly, they are all evil.

Not every action of theirs is necessary evil at face value, but each action of theirs, their very existence, is meant to promote the kingdom of Satan and break down the kingdom of God. Because all their actions are aimed ultimately at destroying the kingdom of God they are evil even if some temporary good comes out of them demons are an order of evil spirits. This order of evil spirits (demons) can be cast out. They take residence in people and places and to set others of evil spirits cannot be cast out. They can only be overthrown. We shall look at their overthrow in the last chapter of this study. Satan as chief and master, can perform the role of all the others. He is the chief of principalities. He is also the chief of powers and so forth. He is the :

1. Ruler of this world (John 12:31)
2. Prince of this world (Ephesians 2:31)
3. Prince of demons (Matthew 12:24).

Satan can himself enter and inhabit a person like the demons do. Satan was around Judas, hardening his heart to the love of Jesus. He injected all kinds of ideas into his mind and when Judas yield to him, the Bible says,

> "So when he dipped the morsel, he gave it to Judas, the son of Simon Iscariot. Then after the morsel, Satan entered into him" (John 13:26-27).

Before, Satan worked on him from outside. Now he was inside and from inside, he started his final task that ended when Judas committed suicide. In that way, he ensured that Judas would be his for ever. In the deliverance ministry, we have encountered demons that have given names an, "The chief" On further questioning they have revealed their identities as lucifer, Satan, the devil, and so on.

In our experience, those have been the most difficult demons to cast out: Often, the smaller demons would complain that they would like to come out and be gone, but the chief would not permit them. Of course, they have often been forced out and the final battle with the demon Lucifer begun and won. Proud people are more susceptible to be inhabited by the devil himself, for when one encounters pride, one encounters the very essence of sin that led to the rebellion and doom of Satan. The proud of heart should do something about it before Satan does something in them. The person, who often acknowledges his pride but does nothing about it, is in some ways admiring himself for being proud. He may say it is bad , but he enjoys it and has no desire to humble himself under the mighty hand of God. He is wooing the devil to come into him. Proud people invariably manifest the presence of demons either in their oppressive or indwelling work by tendencies like self-centredness, excessive concentration on self, being extremely fastidious, hypersensitivity, and so on.

DEMONS : THEIR ORIGIN AND NATURE

Many people believe that demons are the fallen angels that rebelled along with Satan and were therefore cast out of heaven with him. The Bible says,

> *"for if God did not spare the angels when they sinned, but cast them into hell and committed them to pits of nether gloom to be kept until the judgement ..." (2 peter 2:4)*

> *" And the angels that did not keep their own position but left their proper dwelling have been kept by him in eternal chains in the nether gloom until the judgement of that day" (Jude 6)*

> *"Then, he will say to those on his left hand, depart from me, you cursed into the eternal fire prepared for the devil and his angels" (Matthew 25:4).*

Demons are a part of the army of Satan. Although they are bound, they nevertheless. Have limited. Freedom even as the devil has been allowed limited freedom. They are under a head, and constitute part of the satanic kingdom. They have no bodies and are generally invisible. They inhabit some places which they prefer to others. There are haunted houses, forests and the like : these being places where demons make their "home" and therefore congregate there.

Demons are not influences. They are personalities like God's angels. They manifest the following to show that they are not influences:

DELIVERANCE FROM DEMONS

1. They can speak. "And Jesus asked him "what is your name?" He replied "My name is legion; for we are many" (Mark 5:9)
2. They understand. In the reference above they understood Jesus question and answered him.
3. They know how to deal with people. They begged Jesus (Mark 5:12). They did not speak rudely, since they knew that He had authority over them.
4. They can believe to limited extend. *"You believe that God is one; you do well. Even the demons believe - and shudder (James 2:19)*
5. They can choose. *"And he begged him eagerly not to send them out of the country" (Mark 5:10) "And they begged him, "send us to the swine, let us enter them" (Mark 5:12)*
6. They can exercise their wills. *"When the unclean spirit has gone out of a man, he passes through waterless places seeking rest and finding none he says, "I will return to my house from which I came" (Luke 11:24).*
7. They have compassion for each other. *"And when he comes, he finds it swept and put in other. Then he goes and brings seven other spirits more evil than himself, and they enter and dwell there; and the last state of that man, becomes worse than the first" (Luke 11:25-26).*
8. They co-operate with each other. See Luke 11:24-26
9. They know their future fate. "And behold, they cried out, what have you to do with us, O Son of God? Have you come here to torment us before the time?" (Matthew 8:29)
10. They are committed to the glory of Satan, their aim is his overall victory and not just victory in small incidents. They will allow themselves to be cast out by the power of Satan, if they can win something greater by that small defeat. Jesus asked the

Pharisees, " And if I cast out demons by Beelzebub, by whom do your sons cast them out? (Matthew 12:27) Jesus was acknowledging that the sons of the Pharisees indeed cast out demons but they used the power of Satan. I know people who do not belong to God's army; unbelievers, who cast out demons. It is all a plot of Satan to ensure that Satan wins something greater. He will allow a demon to be cast out if by that incident he can re-enforce his kingdom in many lives. He is prepared to lose one and gain five. He is prepared to lose one for one day, but afterwards, gain that one for ever.

Sorcerers and the like, use Satan's power to heal and reveal unknown things, but the overall purpose is to have the person, so that he may be committed to the wrong power and so belong to Satan permanently. No one should just be taken up with a healing that has taken place. The question to ask is, "What is the ultimate condition of the man who is healed? Does he come to Jesus for the greater healing from sin?

DEMONS: THEIR MANIFESTATION

The manifestations of demons, to some extend, are imitations of the manifestations of the Holy Spirit. Most of them are unusual, even as the manifestation of the Holy Spirit are unusual.

The following are some manifestations of the presence of one or more demons in a person:

A)

1. Au uncontrollable talkativeness, sometimes including shouting. At times, the person who has the demon or demons would be talking alone. If you listen, you will think that he is talking to someone who is also talking back to him. The demon which manifests itself in talkativeness, cannot stand any quietude. It must talk even when asked to be quiet, it will still talk out through the person.
2. An uncontrollable reservedness. They will cause the person to keep quiet almost always. The person would enjoy solitude. He could lock up himself in a house for days, alone not because he wants to do anything that needs solitude, but because the demon is happiest in solitude. If people break into the solitude, everything is done to re-establish it.
3. An uncontrollable love of food. The person will eat and eat. He thinks of food. He makes plans about food. He would fall out with you if you did not give him food. He may be fat or thin but he is bound to food in an unusual way. Such a person has an appetite that enjoys the whole range of food possible. It is as if everything must end up in the mouth and stomach.
4. An uncontrollable desire to be noticed. The person who has a demon that manifests itself through the love to be noticed, will do everything to draw attention to himself. His speech, action and all would be centred on being seen. He may even do foolish things to be seen. He may commit a crime, kill, burn himself, and so on, so as to be notice. It does not matter who is talking notice of him. All he is concerned about is that someone is talking notice of him

5. Uncontrollable sexual desire. I once ministered to a man who had gone to bed with over 300 women. He had gone to be with children, mothers and grandmothers. He went to bed with a woman, her daughter and her mother. It was sickening to listen to him as he confessed the atrocious acts of his life. I was so shocked that it took me three days to recover. He was moved, excited by anything in a dress. In addition, he was totally lost in a life of masturbation and also practised homosexuality. I again ministered to a girl, who at 16, could give herself to ten men in one day! There were obviously the manifestations of demons.
6. Uncontrollable anger.
7. An unceasing capacity to lie. Such a demon causes the person to lie to get himself out of some embarrassing situations. He also lies when it is absolutely unnecessary. He lies for fun. He creates lies and enjoys them. Even when he wants to speak the truth, he finds himself lying. He finally begins to believe his lies and cannot distinguish them from the truth.
8. An unusual attachment to the supernatural. I once came in contact with a woman who was a member of six secret (satanic) societies. She, in addition, consulted sorcerers on a weekly basis. She was always visiting one witch doctor after the other. Today she would have a pain in her arm and go to the witch doctor. She would be healed. Next week, there would be pain in her back. She would be back to the witch doctor and then the pain would disappear. Then there would be pains in her head, and so forth. Unfortunately, when I met her, I was

not experienced in the detection of the manifestation of demons. I told her that her that it was contrary to the word of God to go to sorcerers. She was angry and never came to some meetings I was holding. Soon afterwards, the devil arranged an early death for her. So as to have her forever.

9. Uncontrollable movements. The hand, the legs, the head, eyes, vocal cords, the tongue, jaw, muscles, hands, feet, and so on, move on their own. I have found people in prayer meetings whose heads were being shaken by a force that was not theirs. I have seen hands shaking, people grinding teeth as if speaking in tongues. A sister came to our house one day and suddenly the muscles of her leg began to move uncontrollably for about thirty minutes. It was disturbing. I suggested to her that she needed ministry but she instead laughed and stood up and went away. Another sister came to our "Clinic for Spiritual Diseases" for deliverance with her husband who is also a brother in the Lord. As we began to talk to her, she turned her eyes towards me. They were totally turned and were absolutely frightful. This was quite recently. I do not know if I would have continued to stay there with her if I had been alone. I have never seen such looks before. Then I notice another thing. She stretched out her leg and the toes began to move in a certain way. The leg began to twist itself in a horrible way. We were face to face with demons. Thanks be to the Lord that before they went away that night, she was delivered and has remained delivered and is growing in grace. In another incident, a believer was referred to our clinic for deliverance from one of the Pentecostal

churches in the North-West province. She was a woman of about 55 and had been a believer for five years. When she came in, we started to pray. Then she fell down and the demons began to twist her neck. I saw her neck being twisted with full force. She was screaming with pain. We tried to push her neck in the opposite direction but the twisting force of the demon was far stronger. She was in deep agony and I suddenly realized that the demons wanted to strangle her before she was delivered. I cried out to the Lord, prayed in other tongues I asked for immediate help from above. I asked for angels and the Lord sent help immediate help from above. I asked for angels and the Lord sent help immediately, for the twisting action stopped. We were then able to deliver her I once saw a brother move forwards to lay hand s on someone for the baptism into the holy Spirit. His hands and fingers were moving in an uncontrollable way. He was not fit to minister. He needed ministry.

10. Uncontrollable moods. I know people whose moods are so uncontrollable that you can leave them for one minute and when you come back, they have become so different in their moods that you actually feel that you are dealing with a totally different person. These are manifestations that show that someone else other than the person is in control : possibly demons.
11. An unusual commitment to vanity.
12. An usual love of money, things, just to name a few, that borders on idolatry. Such a person will generally prefer things to people. He may sacrifice wife, children, friends or relatives for things. He is always

bargaining in all relationships and his bargains are always on that part of the relationship that involves money and property.
13. An unforgiving spirit.
14. A suspicious spirit.
15. An unusual capacity to forget.
16. A very stubborn will.
17. A very weak will.
18. Uncontrollable emotions. Such a demon would cause the person to become involved in emotional affairs left and rights. Today she may be dying for Mr A. Then, soon she has forgotten Mr A. And suddenly dying for Mr. B. Before that relationship is stabilized, she is no longer interested in B. It is C who is now the hero. She seems to fall in love 100% and to fall out of love 100% in a space of days or Months. She complains of a broken heart but the heart is broken today, healed tomorrow and broken again on the third day.
19. An unusual capacity not to feel.
20. Unusual strength. Demons often manifest unusual strength. Remember one evening when the assembly came together. We asked that any demons present should manifest themselves and commanded them in the name of the Lord Jesus to do so. A young sister of 18 years, who is thin and weighed about 50 kilos, started to speak loudly in other tongues. Then she fell down and rushed under the benches. She stuck there so strongly that we could not pull her out. We had to lift the benches in order to get out. Standing near her was one of the deacons who weighs about 68 kilos. Suddenly, this small girl lifted him up with her one hand and was about to dash

him to the floor when we came to the rescue. It needed three stout men holding her down on each side, for her to be delivered. After she was delivered (it took about 4 hours) we were told the facts. When she was eleven years old. Her grandmother told her that she was engaged to a water spirit. She was therefore to marry no one else. After she had believed , this spirit came one night and took her into the deep ocean and showed her his home. He told her that there was something in her that was standing in the way of their marriage that someone in her was putting him off. He laboured to commit immorality with her but it was a fierce struggle that ended wither victory. the night in which this manifestation took place, he was standing outside the evangelistic Center and calling on her to go with him. When we delivered her, the tongues she spoke ceased. We commanded the spirit never to come back to her Until she was delivered. She was unusually strong. We have seen this over and over. I have received powerful blows from weaklings who under the manifestation of demons, became unusually strong. However, other demons behave differently. There was another case where the girl who was being delivered was so anxious to expose her breasts and other sexual parts. It was perhaps a spirit of immorality or it was a trick of enemy to try and get us to lust after her in our hearts and there fore lose the power to deliver her (power and holiness are vitally linked). We stood firm in the life of holiness into which we had entered by faith in the finished work of the cross and delivered the girl.

Yes, demons can be uncontrollably strong. You will remember the demoniac in the Bible who broke all fetters with he was tied. After deliverance, this supernatural strength normally disappears.

B) Demon manifestation as diseases.

As we shall see in the following chapter, Jesus cast out demons that manifested themselves as the following diseases :

1. Epilepsy.
2. Dumbness and blindness.
3. Infirmity, manifested in a woman not being able to straighten herself, for she was ben over, for over eighteen years.
4. Convulsion

Many of such diseases in the world today are the result of demon inhabitations. Such diseases will not yield to the healing ministry. They will yield to the deliverance ministry. When the demons of diseases are cast out, perfect heath will be restored to the person. It should be noted that not all diseases are demonic in origin. To cast out demons where they do not exist, because a person is sick, is folly.

THE WORK OF DEMONS IN UNBELIEVERS

What is purpose of demons in unbelievers? Their purpose is not just to produce manifestations. Their purpose is to prevent people from coming to a living fait in the Lord Jesus. It is too withstand God's eternal purpose that Jesus should be the first-born of many brethren. If demons prevent a person from coming to the Lord, They have done an excellent job.

Therefore, demons wage war constantly on the unbeliever to prevent him from coming to salvation.

1. They cause him to be spiritually blind. The apostle said,

> *"And even if our gospel is veiled only to those are perishing. In their case, the god of this world has blinded the minds of the unbelievers, to keep them from seeing the light of the gospel of the glory of Christ, who is the likeness of God"* (2corinthians 4:3-4).

The god of this world uses demons to accomplish this by making the unbelievers blind. He makes them blind by causing them to see Jesus:

- as one of many prophets.
- as one of many ways back to God.
- as a good example.

He cause the death of Jesus on the cross to be veiled to the unbelievers

He attacks the doctrine of the substitutionary death of Christ on the cross

He cause them to see Jesus as a good example to be imitated but not as the Saviour to be received.

He blinds them to their sin and its consequences.

He blinds them to the salary of sin which is eternal separation from God in the lake of fire.

He blinds them to the urgency of salvation and deceives them into thinking that they have a lot of time and could repent later on.

2. He deceives them into thinking that God is too good to punish sinners forever.

He deceives them into thinking that God will have mercy on them because they are many.

He deceives some into thinking that all the beautiful girls and musicians will be in the lake of fire and so life there will be enjoyable.

He deceives them into thinking that the life in Christ is boring and monotonous.

He deceives them into thinking that heaven will be boring with many dreary songs.

He deceives them into thinking that because there will be so many sinners in the lake of fire, the punishment shall be less painful.

He deceives them with many other foolish argument

3. He fills them with hatred for the preachers, especially the evangelists.

He prejudices their hearts to what is being preached.

He fills the air with lies about the evangelists:

- Their finances,
- their relationship with people,
- their sexual lives,

- and other things and uses these lies to tell people that they are not living what they are preaching and so it is useless listening to them.

4. He cause them not to thing serious about the meaning of life. He fills them with useless things which preoccupy them e.g:

- football,
- alcohol
- tribal meetings and so on.

He forces one thing after another upon them. He ensures that they are totally taken up with the non essentials and in that way they miss the central issue of life.

5. He forces them to become taken up with secret societies like: Ngondo, Ogboni, Famla, Nyankwe, Obasinjo... By their involvement in these Cameroonian secret societies, their hearts are completely seduced and imprisoned. They, therefore, become the dwelling place of many demons and their damnation is sealed.

6. He woos them to become members of secret societies of foreign origin, like the:

- Rosicrucian order,
- Free Masons,
- Cross and Stars and others, and in this way, they are lost to God completely

7. He gives them faith in one of the religions that guarantees its adherents a place in the lake of fire, like

- Buddhism,
- Baha'i faith,
- Islam,
- Communism,
- and te rest.

In these religions where man is his own saviour, as there is no Saviour and no cross, people are lost permanently.

8. He causes children to be dedicated to some idol by their parents or to be baptized into Satan and as such he holds over them and ensures that they never believe.

9. He makes some into mediums and so their chances of hearing the gospel and believing are greatly reduced.

10. He possesses some unbelievers completely, making some totally mad or in the process, so that they may never be able to respond to the gospel.

11. He cause demons of deafness and blindness to inhabit some and thereby severely reduces their chances of ever hearing the gospel.

12. He cause entire population to remain in illiteracy so that the communication of the world is severely limited. In this way, he causes them never to hear the Gospel.

13. He possesses people and kills them before they believe, in order to ensure that they are his for ever.

The answer to all those attempts and activities of Satan against the Gospel is:

1. People who are truly filled with the Holy Spirit.
2. People who truly walk close to the Lord.

3. People who are willing and able to take up the whole armour of God and to stand against him.
4. People who know what Jesus did on the cross to overthrow all the demons that there are.
5. People who pray.

Demons are at war to prevent people from turning from sin to Christ. The church is at war. With the devil and his servants. In fact, the church is at war. While witnessing to people, sometimes I have felt that they were clearly being blocks from hearing or understanding the Gospel. Of recent, I have learnt to stop and directly command the interfering demons to give way so that the person may hear the gospel. Sometimes, I have commanded the demon of unbelief to leave the person, and then gone on to present the claims of Christ. Sometimes, it has been a demon of distraction causing the person to move from subject without being able to concentrate on the central theme. Sometimes, I have silently commanded that spirit to leave. At other times I have had to speak right aloud. In each case, things have changed as the demon was commanded to stop interfering.

Evangelism is violence on the kingdom of Satan However, in all wars, there are casualties on both sides. I have had many fights in the last eighteen years with the devil. I remember once while I was teaching at Makerere University, Kampala. At a Youth Camp, the Lord had spoken to us about personal evangelism. I dedicated one week to go out from 8am to 12 noon and then from 2pm. To 6pm.cOne day, in one of the parks of Kampala, I saw three young men. I asked them for permission to tell them about the Lord Jesus. Two refused, but one was willing.

DELIVERANCE FROM DEMONS

The other two went away and left me talking to the one who was willing. It was a good time of witnessing and the young man was responding very well to the Gospel. We came right through to the point when he was about to pray and received the Lord Jesus into his life. It is then that one of the swiftest raids of all time took place. The other two young men who had been unwilling to hear the gospel, suddenly rushed upon the one who was about to pray. Lifted him and carried him away as if in a very swift raid. I stood there stunned. I had not foreseen this. I had prayed that he would believe but I had not imagined that such a physical raid was possible and so I did not bother about it. The Enemy saw that loophole which was not covered by prayer and be came in and I lost the battle. I have since learnt to put each aspect of an evangelistic meeting, be it personal evangelism or a crusade, under the blood of the lamb. It is necessary. It works. Glory be to God. The devil and his demons can be out-classed in each encounter, but we must pay the price. Amen.

2

THE ATTACK OF BELIEVERS BY DEMONS

INTRODUCTION

Although demons have free access to unbelievers, they do not bother very much about them. Provided they can prevent them from coming to genuine faith and commitment to the Lord Jesus. So, as far as a person remains in unbelief, Satan's purpose for him is accomplished. He may want to use the one he has kept in unbelief in many other ways but that is a secondary matter. The unbeliever is in some ways, a child of the devil. The Lord Jesus told the pharisees and Scribes of his day,

> *"You are of your father the devil, and your will is to do your father's desires" (John 8:44).*

He again said,

> *"The field is the world, and the good seed means the sons of the kingdom; the weeds are the sons of the devil"* (Matthew 13:38-39).

Because the unbeliever is a son of the devil and demons are soldiers of the devil, demons will not tend to cause great havoc on the sons of their master. Their fury and rage is reserved for the believers, for these are children of God, who is the devil's principal. Enemy. It should be expected that when a person believes in the Lord Jesus, and is thereby transferred from the kingdom of satan into the kingdom of the Lord Jesus, his conflict with demons will then begin. Before, there was harmony between him and the demons, as they served one master, one kingdom and one master's will. Now things are different. There is conflict. There is war. The believer will be attacked by demons and they win to any extent that they are allowed. As you read this, if your sins have been washed in the blood of Jesus and He has given you power to become a child of God, you should know that a price is on you. The devil has put a price on you, a price that failing, hinder you from being all that God saved you for and all that He wants you to be. If you cannot be gotten out of the kingdom of Jesus, He will ensure that although you are in that kingdom, you are rendered as useless as possible.

He has three major things that he can do to believers through the agency of demons. He can:

1. Deceive believers.
2. Oppress believers.
3. Take residence in believers.

It is often difficult to distinguish between an oppression by demons, which mean that the demons are outside the believers but acting upon him, and the taking of residence in believers which means that the demons are acting from inside the believers. Because of this, there is unnecessary disagreement among believers. This need not be so. The most important thing is not whether the demons are acting from inside or from outside. The most important thing is that their activity should be stopped, and the believer delivered. Whosoever is delivered, be it from the demons who oppress him or from a resident demon, is delivered and the Lord has glorify for it. In our understanding of scripture and in our experience in the deliverance ministry, an experience which has involved about one hundred different people in different countries, over a period of ten year, we have dealt with believers who were obviously inhabited by one or more demons. It could be argued that because they had a demon, they were not genuine believers. Well, we thought and we think that they were, even when they had demon in them. We, however, submit to the fact that whether a person has a demon or not, regardless of his confession and commitment, only the Lord knows in an ultimate sense those who are his indeed. The word of God says,

> *"the Lord knows those who are his "and "Let everyone who names the name of the Lord depart from iniquity" (2 Timothy 2:19)*

The many believers, indeed most believers, who have not depart from iniquity may not be the Lord's own. Are you the Lord's own? Have you departed from all the iniquity in your life? If you are still practising, it is an indication that you may be face. You are in danger of being taken over as a habitation of demons.

ATTACK OF THE SOULS OF BELIEVERS BY DEMONS.

Demons concentrate their attacks of believers on their souls and bodies in their attacked just as in the unbeliever. They attack the believer's will making it either very weak so that he cannot stand on decisions he has made, or they make his will so strong and stubborn that even when he is mistaken, he will continue in the path has been chosen. The liberated will of the believer is neither strong nor weak. It is malleable. It can be made to be very strong or ver y soft, depending on the need. It is malleable in the hands of the spirit.

A strong will is not necessarily a blessing. It could be a great curse. The strong-willed person can accomplishments may not be from the will of God. Demons can attack the will, making it out of shape by being too strong or too weak. In either case, it is out of proportion with the overall personality of the person. A strong will under demonic attack can decide to carry out some resolution out of proportion to all else. Demons also attack the will and made it very weak so that the person is able to change his mind one hundred times about the same thing.

He will say. "I will do this. You can count on me." No sooner have you left than another will make a different suggestion and off goes the first decision into the dust bin and the second one becomes that which must be accomplished. It is important for believers to see that this is an attack of demons and that help should be sought and obtained. They are not necessarily inhabited by the demon or demons that are responsible for this. For demons can well perform such a function without taking residence in the person's will.

The same thing is done to the will, can be done to the mind and the emotions. Thus, all three parts of the soul can come under attack. The degree of attack and the extent of the victory that is won by the demons depends on whom they are dealing with. If the person stands his ground and resists the demons, then they will go away. If he lets them have their way, they will stay.

DECEPTION OF BELIEVERS BY DEMONS

A. Demons will attack the world of God and thereby deceive believers.

They do this in four ways:

1. Weakening the authority of Scripture. There are countless demons that are working to tell believers that the Bible is not absolutely reliable and that is should not be taken as it is but, rather, that there should be caution.
2. Distorting the teaching of Scriptures. Demons attack some so that those under attack say, "although that is written, the writer did not mean that. He meant another thing and that thing is ..." Such people read the world and distort it without knowing that they are doing so. They may be very sincere but they are sincerely distorting the word without knowing it. Their minds are attacked and they follow the thoughts of their hearts.
3. Adding to the Scriptures the thoughts of men. Demons have gotten many people to add the thoughts of men to the thoughts of God. This is going on daily in religious and even in Christian o circles. Many of those who do such things hardly realize the fact that they are acting at the command of demons.

4. Putting aside the word of God entirely. There are people who have completely put away what the word of God says about some things. Take as an example, the word of God says that believers are to receive the indispensable anointing from on high and then go out into the work of proclaiming a message they are not qualified to proclaim. The results in many places have been people who have become hardness towards the Gospel of God.

B. Demons will also deceive by attacking the mind of believers.

1. They make suggestions to the mind. For example, one may have a sudden idea flash through one's mind and then he thinks that it is from the Lord. A Bible passage may suddenly be put into the mind by deceiving demons and it is taken as a word of guidance from the Lord. All these are just manifestation s of demonic activities

They may also give visions, voices and special dreams to believers. Many believers will say, "The Lord said to me in a vision that I was praying, a voice spoke to me saying that..." Another may say, "I dreamt that the Lord has asked me to stop my business and become an evangelist. In my dream I saw myself preaching to a very large crowd. This must be the Lord calling me to full time ministry" there could truly be from the Lord. They could equally be the activities of demons. They could be his lies. The fact that a voice is heard during prayer does not necessarily make it the lord's voice. The enemy is a deceiver. He knows that if he speaks prayer, he is most likely to be readily believed, as his voice would be mistaken for God's. And so he succeeds to deceive many believers. The fact that one dreams about becoming a "full time" preacher does not necessarily make the dream be of the Lord. The devil can appear as an angel of Light. If God's will is that you should be in some business, but the devil succeeds to get you to become an evangelist, he has won the battle. God is concerned about his will. He is not concerned about having evangelist who are appointed by demons. Such evangelist may apparently succeed, but they will, in the final analysis, ruin the work of the Lord. Only work that is conceived, initiated and accomplished by God, means anything before him. Only workers who are called, set apart and sent forth by the Lord will do his work. All who sent themselves serve the devil. They are sent by the devil. They are sent out as a result of demonic activity.

A voice can truly say, "thus says the Lord." Anyone who hears such a voice has not heart wrongly. He has possibly heard correctly. The Question however remains to be asked, "Is it indeed the Lord speaking or a demon who has decided to use the Lord's name? Not to face the face the fact is to commit folly.

C. Demons will also deceive by attacking the emotions of believers.

Demons can counterfeit the presence of the Lord and make it an influence or a feeling. Take for example the desire of many people to feel" the Lord. They spend :

- hours,
- days,
- weeks and sometimes.
- monthly,

looking for feelings and emotional experiences. They say, "I did not feel the Lord's presence, so the Lord was not at that meeting." or they can say, "I felt the Lord so near." The problem is that they are doing something that they are not supposed to be doing. Nowhere in doing something that they are not supposed to be doing. Nowhere in the Bible are people encouraged to seek emotional experiences, they will be attacked by demons who will produce "emotions" in them. They will say, " I felt the Lord so near,"but this feeling soon passes away and leaves them no nearer the Lord. Often it leaved them disappointed and discouraged. In that condition of disappointed and discouragement, the enemy can do greater havoc on them.

True feelings can come from the Lord but they come to people who seek the Lord and not to those who seek feelings.

Some believers truly try to induce feeling s in one way or the other. They may say, "praise the Lord," very many times and labour to induce feelings this way. During the ministry of laying on of the hands for the baptism into the Holy Spirit, some breathe very deeply or shake or scream. All such thing s are activities of the flesh that which can only be produced by the Holy Spirit. Such actions make room for demons to act. I once met a brother who told me that he was baptized into the Holy Spirit. His presence caused a lot of uneasiness in my spirit. I asked him how he had gotten baptized into the Holy Spirit and he told me that at the particular meeting, he was told to say, " praise the Lord, "One thousand times and as fast he could. He started to say "praise the Lord, praised the Lord, Praise the Lord…" and somewhere along the line he found he was speaking in another tongue Yes indeed he spoke with another tongue but it was not a tongue given by demons as he tried to use carnal methods to acquire that which only the holy Spirit gives. By trying to bypass his mind with his "praise the Lord," he had opened room for demons and they took over and acted fast.

D. Believers who are true, faithful and honest, can be deceived by Satan and his demons for the following reasons

First of all, when a person turns from sin and receives the Lord Jesus, he becomes a child of God. He is, however, still a spiritual baby and does not posses full knowledge either of God, himself or the devil. In all three areas, there is ignorance and where there is ignorance, deception is possible. A sincere believer can, therefore, be deceived.

Secondly, deception has to do with the mind. It means that a wrong thought is admitted into the mind, under the deception that it is truth. Deception is based on ignorance and not on moral character.

This means that a faithful believer; faithful and true to the Lord up to the extent of the knowledge that he has received, is still open to being deceived in the sphere where he is ignorant. During the East African revival, some believers, sincere but ignorant, were led to believe that since clothes came with the fall, if a person was saved, he was no longer in the condition that made clothes necessary. So, on a Sunday morning, seven such believers (four men and three women) walked into a church service as naked as they were a birth. It was a shock and scandal to many and some hardened their hearts to the Gospel. Some others said that they had "Crucified the old man" and were totally free from sin and so could not be tempted to sin at all. To prove that they were beyond the reach of sin, they said that brothers and sisters in the Lord could lie on the same beds and since the old man was totally crucified, nothing would happen. They did lie with each other and to the disgrace of God's glorious name, shameful things took place. They were sincere but ignorant and, therefore, demons deceived them.

Thirdly, the thought that God will protect a believer from being deceived, is a lie. In fact, it is the devil's lie because it throws a man off guard and makes a man ignore the fact that there are conditions to be fulfilled by man before he can be fully protected by the Lord. If full protection by the Lord was automatic, Then no believer would :

- be deceived,
- sin or
- be attacked by disease

God will not do anything in the place of man, but God will do much in co-operation with him. When someone says, "I will not think . God will think for me," he opens himself up to deceiving demon, for nowhere has God promised to do the thinking for the believer. The Bible invites to think. The word of God say:

> "what do you think," (Matthew 18:12)

> "what do you think of the Christ ? Whose Son is he' (Matthew 22:42)

> "...to think with sober judgment, each according to the measure of faith which God has assigned him" (Romans 12:3)

THE ATTACK OF BELIEVERS BY DEMONS

"Think about these things" (Philippians 4:8)

The same think applies to the will. God has nowhere promised to will for us. If a person refuses to will and says that the Lord will will for him, he opens himself up to demons. Each believer has the responsibility to think and to will. God will not choose for you. You must choose for yourself. You must find out what God's will is. This is an active process. Then you must choose that will deliberately and thus consciously make his will your will. If any believer runs away from performing these legitimate functions of the soul, leaving them to the Lord, God will not do anything about them. Rather, demons will take over and begin to make decisions for him.

God has not promised that He would make up for the believer's ignorance of :

- God,
- himself,
- the Enemy or
- the World, for instance.

God has nowhere promised that all the dreams of a believer will originate in Him. God has nowhere promised that the sudden remembrance of a Bible passage, by a believer, will be from Him. Those who study the Word consistently and in an organized manner, are less likely to be deceived than those who "wait" for sudden revelation of passages for guidance.

That God's children can be sincere, consecrated, prayerful and yet ignorant and therefore deceived, is confirmed by the following incidents:

DELIVERANCE FROM DEMONS

1. In Yaounde, Cameroon, an important figure in the nation died. A well educated, highly placed Christian woman of about forty-five years who had been a believer since she was eighteen, heard a voice that spoke in the name of the Lord, asking her and another Christian woman of thirty-two who had been a believer for twelve years, to go to the grave where the dead man had been buried and pray and the dead man would be raised from the dead. They went to the grave, prayed and nothing happened. They had heard and obeyed lying demons and not the Lord.

2. Fourteen years ago, the author, a doctoral student in Chemistry and another brother, were praying together shortly after they had been baptized into the Holy Spirit (and were certainly seeing many people saved as a result of their baptism into the Holy Spirit). The author, who was the older and more mature of the two spiritually, heard a voice that said, "Be alert. The Lord wants to talk to you." The other brother got a pen and a notebook and began to write out the detailed instructions that were supposed to come from the Lord. The voice commanded that we were to go to a brother who was crippled. We would find him sitting at a particular place in his room. It was to be at 5.00 pm. and we would command him to be healed in the name of the Lord and he would be healed. We rejoiced at God's great goodness to us and prayed with joy for the rest of the night. The next day, we anxiously waited for the hour. At 4 pm, we met and prayed together. At exactly 5.00pm we were at the sick brother's room. He was not at the position

where we had been told that we would find him. He was not in his room at all. Had we been more knowledgeable, we would have recognized the fact that we had been deceived since he was not at the place where the voice had told us that he would be. We went looking for him but we did not find him. Later on, he came in and we told him the "good news" and sent out his room-mate who was an unbeliever, telling him that by the time he came back his room-mate would be perfectly normal. We, then, asked our brother to sit at the place and in the posture in which we had been told we would find him. Then we gave the word of command as had been given us. Nothing happened. We repeated it and again nothing happened. We asked our brother to exercise faith and laid hands on him and prayed to total exhaustion, and still nothing happened. We then held the brother's sick leg and pulled it out for perfect health in the name of Jesus, but nothing happened. After three hours, we not only missed the special dinner that was given in the hall that day with plenty of chicken, in addition, we were totally exhausted, discouraged and frustrated. We did not understand where we had gone wrong. I understood later on. We had heard the voice of demons and obeyed it and since demons only deceive, we had been left where we were and had brought much dishonour to the Lord's name. We were both baptized into the Holy Spirit. We were both consecrated. We were not living in any known sin. We were fruitful witnesses and given to much prayer. The voice had actually spoken during prayer and yet it was the voice of demons. We were ignorant then of the fact that demons can speak in the name of the Lord. Because we were ignorant, our obvious spirituality did not shield us from being deceived.

From these examples and many others involving sincere believers, we insist that, in order not to be deceived by the words of lying demons, the believer should test all thoughts, visions, dreams, revelations, voice, and so on, by:

1. Their harmony with the Word of God in its full body of truth, and not just a small part of it. This makes a knowledge of the full body of revealed truth a must for all believers.
2. Their attitude to the cross and sin. There are people who claim to have received the gift of tongues from the Holy Spirit, yet they confess that they worship "holy Mary" better now in other tongues. Their tongues must originate from the Enemy. The Holy Spirit cannot give utterance in tongues to be used to worship a human being. The utterance from Him will bring worship and honour to the Lord and to Him alone.

The ultimate purpose of the devil, working through demons and his other agents, is to hide, distort, misuse, or put aside the revelation of God concerning the cross of Calvary where Satan was overthrown by Jesus and where freedom was obtained for all captives.

All that we have said about deception by demons can take place without the demons taking residence in the believer. They inject these ideas from outside the believer.

THE ATTACK OF BELIEVERS BY DEMONS

All believers should note that voices have three possible origins:

- The Lord the Holy Spirit,
- The human spirit or soul i.e. self,
- Wicked spirits or demons.

Each time a voice is heard or a dream is had, or a vision is seen, the origin should be checked. If it originates from the Holy Spirit, it should be obeyed. If the origin is from self, or evil spirits, or demons, it should be rejected. Believers should walk close to the Lord, and test everything. They should know the Word, and walk by it. They should not be given to a spirit of believing everything. They should consult the more mature ones before they move in new directions.

OPPRESSION BY DEMONS

Demons do not only deceive. They oppress without taking residence in the believer.

Demons may oppress in the form of nightmares. All night, one has frightful dreams and wakes up restless. One may dream that one was being chased by a wild animal, or a snake. The purpose of this is to cause restlessness. One then wakes up broken and tired, and the purpose of sleep has been destroyed.

Demons may also oppress the believer by making him weary for no reason. They may make a believer feel that something is going to go wrong, just to cause restlessness.

Demons may oppress the believer by attacking his :

- finances,
- property,
- time,
- career,
- relationships,
- wife,
- husband,
- parents,

just to name a few.

The purpose of these attacks is to distract the believer from the central issue of serving the Lord and walking with Him, to the side-issues that are outlined above. The believer may find that demons arrange for someone to hit his car just as he is driving to go and preach the gospel. They may cause planes to break down when there is an important flight in view. The whole purpose is to cause delay and weariness in the spirit.

Demons concentrate on causing division among believers. They will cause some believers to concentrate on some secondary doctrinal issue, to the exclusion of the other major teachings of the Word. By this concentration on secondary issues, one is forced to be separated from the others and stand alone, thereby being open for further destructive attacks from demons. The devil's policy is "divide and rule." He will make believers who are involved in some unimportant disagreement, to each think that the fault is with the other party. Demons, working through the uncrucified flesh of believers, make each to see the fault of the others while being completely blind to their own. Demons make believers to think that the solution will come when the other person has changed. This is part of their oppressive warfare.

THE ATTACK OF BELIEVERS BY DEMONS

Demons concentrate on trying to destroy the marriages of Christians, especially the marriages of Christian leaders. Some years ago, a number of satanists in Southern Africa each fasted for 40 days. They asked only one thing from their master the devil. They said to him, "Destroy the marriages of Christian leaders." It would seem that thousands upon thousands of demons were released by Lucifer, against the marriages of Christian leaders in answer to that special fast and prayer.

I will quote just three examples:

1. Some years ago I was involved in big evangelistic meetings in a country whose name I prefer to withhold. After one of the evening meetings during which the power of the Lord had been specially manifested, I continued counselling until late in the night. At around midnight, a respectable lady came in and started talking to me. She told me how bad her marriage was and all the bad things that her husband had done to her all through the years. The things that she said, painted a picture of a very wicked person, so I thought that I needed to meet him and witness to him so that there may be hope. She concluded by saying that she had thought of suicide many times. When I asked her what her husband's name was, she was surprised. She did not know that I had not recognized her. Then she, surprisingly, gave me his name and I almost collapsed with shock. He was the leading man of God in that town, the president of a flourishing Pentecostal denomination and the chief organizer of the meetings at which I was speaking. When I recovered my composure, I said to her, "Sister, this is an attack of demons. There is no other explanation." I then prayed and commanded all the demons who were set loose against that family to depart forthwith and I pleaded that the blood of the Lord would

DELIVERANCE FROM DEMONS

protect their marriage from that moment and into all of the future. Demons were at work but Jesus is the answer.

2. I received two letters this week. One is from a man of God and the other from a woman of God. The first letter reads,

> *My beloved brother Zach,*
>
> *It is with tears that I am writing this letter to you, Ever since last year, my wife and I have lived in constant conflict. It seems as if it is totally impossible for us to live in peace even for one day. We can't agree on anything. We don't even do anything in common. We have really become two complete strangers. We can't pray or read the Bible together. I dare not speak of our sexual life. We last met many months ago. My wife is very, very miserable. I'm really sorry for her. It breaks my heart. In fact, I'm not wrong to say that our marriage finished long ago, I have lost my place in her heart, same as she has lost hers in mine... All this has had a disastrous effect on the church and the work. I am paralysed. Who will roll away the stone? My beloved brother, I am sorry that I have to break your heart with such a letter. I have long since tried to avoid it, but I thought it would definitely be good for you to know now. Perhaps, you can help. Thank you for your prayers..."*

When I first read this letter I burst into tears. This couple loves the Lord more than any other couple I know anywhere in God's world, but see! I just saw that it was an attack of demons and so I stopped crying and entered into vigorous intercession with words that are known, then with words that are unknown, then without words. I spoke to the demons that were sent on this family, in the name of Jesus, and commanded them to leave. I separated them each from the other and separated them from Satan and in that way I

THE ATTACK OF BELIEVERS BY DEMONS

sowed confusion in their midst by breaking down their communication. I, then, asked each one to leave in the name of the Lord Jesus. It was a fierce battle and I felt the weight of it in my soul and body. This went on for about an hour and then the burden left me. I believe that the battle is won and that I will receive another letter soon to tell me that things have changed radically. I believe that they will not be able to tell what has happened. They will just discover that the cloud has rolled away; that the Holy Spirit has rolled away the stone. This is conflict with demons but it is also victory in the name of the Lord Jesus, I have also put that couple and that marriage under the precious blood of the Lord. Things will go better from now on.

3. I have no liberty to share the second letter with you and so I will just go on.

Demons also oppress believers by causing all kinds of lies and gossips to be spread about them that vex the spirit and dislocate spiritual action. Most gossips are people under the attack of demons. Apart from gossips, there are liars in the church. They know that liars will not enter the kingdom of God but they cannot help lying.

Because there is warfare, demons are bound to be always seeking for an opportunity to attack. What is the best way to avoid being attacked? I believe that there is one place where the power of demons is reduced to nothing. That place is the blood of the Lord Jesus. Those who hide under the blood of Jesus and keep all who are theirs under the blood of Jesus, as well as all that is theirs, will find that the attempts of demons to attack them and theirs, are not effective.

DELIVERANCE FROM DEMONS

It is no use praying in a general way. General prayers are not as effective as very specific ones. I am learning to put all that I am and all that I have, as well as all that I want to do, under the blood of Jesus, daily. I pray in the following way every morning: "Lord Jesus, I put the following under Your blood and therefore, out of reach of all the demons sent out to attack them:

- My will
- My body,
- My ambitions,
- mind,
- health,
- moods,
- emotions,
- looks,
- job,
- thoughts,
- plans,
- My wife
- My wife's health,
- daughter Ruth
- her job,
- son Paul,
- moods
- son Stephen,
- relationship with
- daughter Eli,
- You and others,
- son John
- our car,
- daughter Mary,
- our house,

THE ATTACK OF BELIEVERS BY DEMONS

- all our property,
- The assembly in Yaounde,
- The funds of the assembly
- The Elders,
- The teaching ministry of the
- The deacons,
- assembly.
- The deaconesses,
- The evangelistic ministry of the assembly,
- The prayer ministry of the assembly,
- The assemblies in the other places, which are a part of my ministry and their leaders and members.
- Our missionary in Chad,
- The Zach Fomum ministry,
- Joseph Mouafo
- Ernest Nzima and
- Jean Ngomba,
- The tracts,
- The books,
- The cassettes,
- The funds,
- My special friends
- The other workers,
- My other friends,
- The building,
- My co-workers,
- My writing ministry,
- My role as a husband
- My role as a father,
- My evangelistic ministry,
- My role as a university teacher,
- My church planting ministry,
- My teaching ministry,

- My role as a spiritual leader,

I put these things under the blood of the Lord and I believe that the attempts of demons to reach them and destroy them would be futile for that day. In this way, I have freedom from the oppression of demons.

There are times when I sense in my spirit that demons are about to attack someone or some place. I take that person or that place in particular, and build a wall of protection with the blood of Jesus around it, in a very specific way. I bring up every small aspect in detail and cover it with the blood. In this way I am able to protect believers who are near and far, and aspects of God's work that are near and far.

INHABITATION OF A BELIEVER BY A DEMON

We have seen that demons can deceive and oppress believers. We want to look now into the matter of a demon residing in a believer. Before we go on, we want to state clearly that all evil spirits and demons were defeated by the Lord Jesus on the cross.

> "He disarmed principalities and powers and made a public show of them, triumphing over them in his cross" (Colossians 2:15).

Because of the triumph of Christ on the cross, evil spirits and demons have no legal grounds to remain in anyone who belongs to Christ. Demons know that fact, but they will not just leave. They will stay for as long as it is possible for them to stay. If forced out, they will leave. A person who has a demon or demons is not automatically delivered the moment he receives the Lord Jesus. The power to be delivered is available, but the demon that was in the person stays until someone uses the power of the Lord to send away the demon.

We notice in the Lord's deliverance ministry that demons did not cry out and depart immediately He came into the presence of the person who had the demon. In each case, He had to command the demon to go out of the person. When He did, the demon invariably left the person.

In our day, when someone comes to receive the Lord Jesus, many people do not bother to set him free from any demons that he may have. They just go on and lead him to a prayer of repentance and commitment to Christ. What would happen with any demon that was in the person before then? The demon would continue to stay in the person, even though the Holy Spirit has taken residence in the person's human spirit and given him power to become a child of God.

Look at it in another way. If a person has a blind demon and he repents and believes in the Lord Jesus, is his blindness automatically healed? No. The blindness, that is evidence of the presence of a demon, will remain until the demon is cast out. Then the blindness will immediately disappear.

It may be asked, "How can the Holy Spirit dwell in a person who has a demon causing blindness?" The answer is that the blindness that is a manifestation of demonic presence needs not prevent the Holy Spirit from coming into the person. The Holy Spirit comes to dwell not in the person's body, not even in his soul but in his spirit. He can dwell in the person's spirit while a demon has control of the person's eyes.

We can also ask, "How can the Holy Spirit come and dwell in a person who is sick?" We know that sickness is the work of the devil and that the Son of God took all our sickness with Him in His suffering and that by His stripes we were healed. Although that work was done, we have to face the fact that there are many people who are sick before they are converted who remain sick after they are converted. There are others who become sick only after they are converted. In the matter of sickness, Jesus Christ who is Perfect Health lives in a believer whose body may be crushed and broken by sickness and diseases. Is that not abnormal that Perfect Health should dwell in a sick and broken body? It is abnormal but real. It will continue to be abnormal but real until the church fully comes into her right of perfect health or until the believer's body is redeemed at the second coming of the Lord. When that happens, the abnormality of the Lord who is Perfect Health, living in diseased bodies, will stop. Similarly, the church should wake up to her full possibilities and potentials in the deliverance ministry, and cast out all demons that people had before they were led to the Lord.

A person may indeed have life like Lazarus had when coming out of the tomb. Nevertheless, he may be bound, needing that the brethren should unbind him. The Lord Jesus imparted life to Lazarus but He did not unbind him. He left it to the disciples to do so.

Today, some will have life imparted to them but they will be bound by grave clothes. It is the church's responsibility to unbind them.

Are you still worried about how a believer can have a demon? Let us look at the matter of sin. Can a believer sin? The answer is "yes" This means that the Holy Spirit will have to live in a body that has committed sin. Can you imagine that

THE ATTACK OF BELIEVERS BY DEMONS

the Holy Spirit actually lives in a believer at the moment when the believer is:

- lying
- committing gluttony
- committing immorality,
- and all the other sins?

The thought of it is very horrible - the Holy Spirit indwelling a sinful body. This sounds a terrible contradiction in terms but it it nevertheless real in Christian experience. Even if the immorality was committed only in thought, it would mean that at the time when it was committed, the soul of the believer committed this dreadful sin while the Holy Spirit dwelt in the spirit of that believer. This sad contradiction is as real as when the Holy Spirit has to dwell for some time in a body that has one or more demons.

Even if a person was thoroughly delivered at the moment he was converted, what happens if he should backslide? In the backslidden condition, he may be open for demons to come and dwell in him again. I have never seen the ministry of deliverance offered to a backslider. Often, he is just prayed for. This means that if some demon had left him when he believed, the same demon could be back with seven others when he backslides, making a more serious deliverance ministry a must after the person comes back to the Lord. The Lord Jesus said,

> "When the unclean spirit has gone out of a man, he passes through waterless places seeking rest; and finding none he says, "I will return to my house from which I came, and when he comes, he finds it swept and put in order. Then he goes and brings seven other spirits

more evil than himself, and they enter and dwell there; and the last state of the man becomes worse than the first" (Luke 11:24-26).

Yes, a person may be completely delivered at the beginning of his Christian life, but he needs to continue to walk with the Lord, so that the demons that were in him at the beginning, plus others that are more wicked, do not come into him later on. The Lord Jesus found it necessary to command that demons should leave someone and never come back. Today, deliverance is either totally lacking in many segments of the Body or those who carry it out forget that the demons can come back. Jesus said,

"You dumb and deaf spirit, I command you, come out of him, and never enter him again" (Mark 9:25).

We know, from hard-earned experience in the deliverance ministry over the last ten years, that demons do come back. For many years, I did not myself know that I had to command the demon(s) never to enter the person again. We have found that if people were delivered and they went back to grave deeds of darkness like sexual immorality, magic, sorcery, just to name a few, demons often came back and the second deliverance was even more difficult than the first. We have found the same thing with healing. The disease sometimes came back and the condition of the person was worse than it was at the beginning. Jesus told one of the people He had healed,

"See, you are well! Sin no more, that nothing worse befall you" (John 5:14).

THE ATTACK OF BELIEVERS BY DEMONS

We know in our own experience with the deliverance of some people, that the deliverance ministry takes days or weeks or months. The person often repents and receives the Lord at the beginning. The ministry then starts and he is only partially delivered. He is already a believer because he has received the Lord of glory. Between the time of his partial deliverance and the time of his full deliverance, he is a believer with demons resident in him.

As we saw clearly in the ministry of Jesus, there were certain diseases which were manifestations of the presence of demons. The person was healed immediately the demon or demons were cast out. It is folly to think that, today, there are no believers whose diseases are of demonic origin and the need is for deliverance and not for healing. The very thought of it betrays the fact that this is a trick of demons in order to avoid being detected and cast out.

We warn that a believer who habitually lives in sin is inviting demons to come and live within him. We also warn that any believer who just says that because he is a believer, demons cannot enter into him because Jesus is living in him, may just be being simple- minded. Why does such a one not go about anyhow and not take care to walk in holiness and say, "Because Jesus lives in me I will not fall into sin?" Why does that one not say, "Because I am a believer, I can do anything I like; I will not fall sick, because Jesus the Healer dwells in me?" Not to be on full guard is to commit folly.

We know that the devil is on the move, going to and fro, up and down in all the earth. He prowls around like a roaring lion, seeking someone to devour. Demons, like their master, may be expected to be going to and fro, and walking up and down the earth, seeking whom to devour. This means that anyone who is not protected or any areas that are not protected, are open to them and they will do what they can to get in. Remember that it is warfare. The demons want to get in. Jesus is inside the believer. Jesus is greater than all demons. However, Jesus will not protect the believer without the believer's co-operation. He commands us to watch - to be alert. He will not watch for us but He will watch with us. He will be alert with us but He will not be alert for us, on His own. He will not do what we must do ourselves. This means that even though the Lord Jesus dwells in the believer, He will not automatically protect the believer from diseases, sin and demons. The believer must exert himself. This world is training ground for rulership with Him in the millennial and eternal kingdoms. It would be poor training if He let us relax while He did for us and in us the things that we are supposed to do in co-operation with Him. Yes, there is war. Demons will use the slightest opportunity that they have to enter into believers if they can. Such an opportunity is provided by deliberate and repeated indulgence in some sin like lying, gluttony, anger, pride and laziness, and so on. Where there is deliberate and repeated sin, the believer is impotent over demons, for by sin, he has taken their side and is fighting with them and for them. Where then is his protection?

A BELIEVER CANNOT BE POSSESSED BY DEMONS.

A believer may have a demon that holds part of his personality or body under control. He may have a demon of fear, or a dumb demon or a dumb and blind demon. These demons only hold sway over part of his person but the rest of his personality or body functions normally. The believer can continue to carry out his normal life although handicapped in that area where the demon holds sway. For example, a believer with a demon of lying may lie hopelessly and endlessly. He will make resolutions that he will not lie. He will pray and fast about it. He will reckon himself dead to sin and alive unto God and then he will unconsciously just continue to lie. In his sexual life, he may be very pure with no impure thoughts whatsoever. He may pray fervently and deeply. He may give to the Lord and be active in serving Him. He is not possessed. He has a demon. When the demon of lying or the lying spirit is cast out, the person would be instantly freed from lying.

A demon possessed person has all of his personality under the control of demons. He cannot relate to the Lord in any real way. Believers cannot be in that condition unless they have totally abandoned the Lord and have denied the faith.

We conclude that a believer can have a demon or demons. He need not have them but they can be there. Their presence in some believers is real but unnecessary. Those who once believed, like the seed on the rocky soil or the thorny soil, continue apparently as believers even though vital fellowship with the Lord is absent. They can have a demon. They can even be possessed by demons. Believers should walk close to the Lord, seek deliverance if they ever backslide and then walk without fear of having demons reside in them.

EXCUSES USED BY DEMONS.

Demons use the following reasons to cover grounds and continue to live in the believer:

1. It is divine.

DELIVERANCE FROM DEMONS

2. It is sin.
3. It is a disease.
4. It is a physical condition.
5. It is a natural condition.
6. It is temperamental.
7. It is hereditary
8. It is a special revelation.
9. It is a special vision from God.
10. It is special for the end time.
11. It is a special gift from the Lord for our special needs

With these excuses, they are often allowed to continue to stay and thereby gain and establish further grounds. The effect of demons in believers include the following (many of these signs are also the result of demonic oppressions).

1. General weakness that cannot be traced to any organic fault by medical examination.
2. The lack of ability to fast and pray. The person's entire being revolts against fasting, and as for prayer, there is neither desire nor power to concentrate.
3. Constant irritability manifested in impatience and restlessness.
4. Unteachability.
5. Prejudice.
6. An exaggerated view of self:
7. Upwards leading to pride,
8. downwards leading to an inferiority complex.
9. Lack of spiritual vision.
10. Unholy laughter.
11. An excessive tendency to weep or laugh.
12. An unusual capacity not to feel.

13. Constant depression.
14. Grossly unstable moods.
15. Gross lack of capacity for self-discipline even after repeated and sincere efforts.
16. Uncontrollable self-centredness.
17. A spirit of division.

DISTINGUISHING BETWEEN THE WORKS OF THE FLESH AND THE MANIFESTATION OF DEMONS IN BELIEVERS.

It is folly to attribute every fault in believers to demons. This itself would be a work of demons, for when things are confused, they take advantage of them. Definite activities of the old man are found in believers. How is one to distinguish these from manifestations of demons? Take, for example, lust, gluttony and anger. How can one tell whether or not it is from the flesh?

The best answer lies in the spiritual gift of discernment of spirits. This gift is indispensable for anyone who wants to take the deliverance ministry seriously. It can be disastrous to tell someone who has no demon that he has one. On the other hand, there are many believers who think that they have demons whereas they indeed have none. Many people want to run away from taking responsibility for their sins, co-operating with the Holy Spirit, repenting and forsaking them and entering into the victory of the Lord. They prefer to say they have a demon and thereby push the blame for their action on the demon. In one school, a girl said to us, "It is true that I lied but it is not my fault. It is the demon of lying in me." I replied, "You are responsible for your lie even if you push the responsibility on demons. You are responsible for any demons in you." It is easier to blame demons for the lust that a person enjoys, rather than take the responsibility to acknowledge it as sin, confess it, forsake it and seek to be delivered from it and be filled with the Holy Spirit.

It is better to consider a fault like the ones outlined as excuses used by demons to gain grounds and the others as activities of the flesh. The flesh cannot be cast out. There is a four-step process to dealing with the activities of the flesh.

Step one :

> "Set your mind on the things that are above and not on things that are earthly" (Colossians 3:2).

Step two :

> "Seek the things that are above" (Colossians 3:11).

This is active.

Step three:

> "Put to death what is earthly in you: fornication, impurity, passion, evil desire and covetousness, which is idolatry" (Colossians 3:5).

Step four :

> "Be renewed in the spirit of your mind" (Colossians 4:23).

Step five :

> "Put on the new nature, created after the likeness of God in true righteousness and holiness" (Ephesians 4:24).

THE ATTACK OF BELIEVERS BY DEMONS

If your problem is an activity of the flesh, things will change as you deal with it and in the way outlined above. It will help if you couple each step with fasting, prayer and Bible study. This should lead to deliverance from that sin or sinful attitude.

If after these means of grace have been employed and you find freedom in many areas of your life except one or two, you are possibly dealing with a demon. The thing about the activity of demons that is striking is that when they are in a believer, that one may manifest much grace and spiritual progress in the Lord in many areas of his life. She may be a woman of prayer, who gives generously to the work and actively witnesses, but she may have an uncontrollable temper. The temper may be there even after many years in the Lord, and its manifestation may be just as violent as when one was in the world. Or it could be a man with a clear grasp of Scripture. He may be tender and compassionate but when it comes to money, the person is totally controlled by it. It could be a demon of gluttony. The person may be serious and able in all areas of his life. He may even hate his ugly, shapeless body and make many resolutions to change, but when he sees food, he will forget all his resolutions until all of it is buried in his stomach. Because demons do not yield to discipline and self-control, things like fasting and Bible reading that aid discipline have no power over them. The man will fast and pray and yet continue to overeat. He has a demon of gluttony. He must deliver himself or be delivered by another or by others.

THE DELIVERANCE OF A BELIEVER WHO HAS A DEMON

In the healing ministry, a believer can be healed through the ministry of someone with the gift of healing or through another believer acting in faith. A person can also claim his healing personally and directly from the Lord, unaided by anyone. The same thing applies to the baptism into the Holy Spirit. One can receive the baptism into the Holy Spirit through the laying on of the hands of another Spirit-filled person or one can, on his own, ask Jesus the Baptizer to baptize him into the Holy Spirit.

Can the same principle apply to the deliverance of a believer from a demon? I believe so. Mr Basham in his book, "<u>Deliver us from evil</u>" suggests the following:

1. **Commitment to Christ.** The promises of the New Testament are for those who belong to Jesus Christ. Therefore, personal deliverance must begin with surrender to Jesus Christ the Deliverer. Be sure that you have fully received Jesus Christ as your Saviour.
2. **Forgive others.** Forgive your husband, wife, son, daughter, mother, father, co-worker, pastor, elder, deacon, and all others. Forgive everyone whose name stirs feelings of bitterness or hostility in you. Forgive everyone whose name causes you pain. Pray and say, "Lord, I forgive.... and ...." Decide now to do it and do it now. You do not have to wait for feelings of forgiveness. Will it and accomplish it irrespective of your feelings.

3. **Renounce all known sin in your life.** Confess and forsake them and claim the cleansing power of the blood of Christ.
4. **Identify the demon.** If you have many demons in you, you have to deal with them one after another. If you do not know which demon to start with, ask it to give its name. Its identity will impress itself forcibly on your mind.
5. **Renounce the spirit by name.** Say, "In the name of Jesus I renounce the demon of ...... "If you have no assurance that the renunciation is thorough, you should repeat it.
6. **Command the demon to leave in the name of the Lord.** You should speak to it clearly but you do not need to shout. As you command it to leave, often, there will be physical manifestations which will cease when the demon has left. Identify and cast out the next demon until your total deliverance has been achieved. End with praise and thanksgiving to Jesus the Deliverer without whom your deliverance would have been impossible.

If you still have a problem with the fact that a believer could have a demon, let me ask you a few questions:

1. Have you ever encountered demons in an unbeliever? If you have never seen demon manifestation in unbelievers, you are unlikely to see them in believers. Something must be wrong with your ministry and person, for if the power of the Lord were fully at work in you, that power would force demons to manifest themselves.

DELIVERANCE FROM DEMONS

2. Have you ever cast out any demons from unbelievers? If you have never cast out any demons from unbelievers then you are not equipped to carry out deliverance of believers and you should be thankful that God has so far spared you from an encounter with demons that could overpower you.
3. Have you ministered to believers who were deceived or oppressed by demons? If you have, then you will soon encounter demons that are resident in believers. The chances are that you might have thought that the demons were oppressing from outside, whereas they were really manifesting themselves from inside.
4. Have you sorted out the matter of the possibility of a believer having a demon with the Lord or you have taken the position of others? For many years I opposed the brethren who were involved in the deliverance ministry in Uganda. I myself was quite acquainted with the deliverance of unbelievers. I had fought for two hours with the demon of insanity in a student in Busoga college, Mwiri and seen him gloriously delivered and healed immediately the demon left. I had also carried out some deliverances around as I evangelised. I well remember one evening when I began to witness to an intelligent man of about 40 at Makerere University. He was quiet and calm and responded very well to the Gospel until we got to the place where he had to receive the Lord Jesus as his Saviour and Lord. Then things suddenly changed. He started to scream and shout like a madman. I was, at first, frightened and as I prayed, I recognized that I was face to face with a demon or demons. The man continued screaming

and shouting. I took authority over the evil spirit in the name of the Lord and commanded it to leave the man. He continued to scream. I commanded the spirit to leave the man in the name of Jesus and laid my hands on the man and began to pray with the spirit. As I prayed, the screaming and shouting began to subside, until it stopped altogether. I asked the man what was happening to him but he could not explain. He was quiet and calm and so I led him to the Saviour who died for him and who had just delivered him. Yet, I continued to oppose anyone who delivered believers. There came a time in my own ministry to believers where the obvious manifestation of demons were seen in people who had believed many years before and were walking with the Lord. In one case at a meeting for the baptism into the Holy Spirit. A believer began to shout and cry like a madman and soon he was foaming. I first thought that it was epilepsy but I had a witness in my spirit that deliverance was needed. We delivered him and I had to choose between facing the fact that he was a believer who had a demon or that he had never believed. I took the matter up with the Lord and withdrew to seek the Lord with prayer and fasting. The Lord spoke clearly to me. I know a believer can have a demon or demons. I have delivered many. At the moment, there are three outstanding cases of believers of some years standing that need to be delivered. My preliminary attempts have failed. One of them is a sister who believed about four years ago and has led some people to the Lord who are going on with Him. She started by saying that the Lord had told her that we had made a mistake not to worship Mary as well as the Lord. Then it continued and now she is in bad shape. There are two other cases. I have not yet found the secret to their deliverance. They are believers or I believe they are believers, but they have a demon or demons. But by God's grace, they will be delivered as the other ones have been delivered and are going on with the Lord.

5. If you see the manifestation of demons in anyone, deliver him, regardless of whether you think that he is a believer or an unbeliever. If you hold that anyone who has a demon is not a believer, deliver him and then lead him to the Lord. Do not run away from delivering people by hiding behind the thought that no believer can have a demon.

6. Do demon-possessed people scream, shout, fall down and foam in your meetings? Do these things happen in your evangelistic meetings and in other meetings where unbelievers are present? If they do not happen, could it be that you lack something that ought to cause them to scream and react? When they saw the Lord, they reacted. Why not you? Why do they not react? Is your world of ministry that one in which demons do not exist at all? What type of world is that? What type of ministry is that? Do the words of the Lord that the sign of casting out demons would follow those who believe not apply to you, or you are an exception? Think and pray about it. Where there is real spiritual power and not just noise, demons will react and manifest themselves. This is normal.

3

THE MINISTRY OF JESUS TO DEMON - ATTACKED PEOPLE

INTRODUCTION

The Lord Jesus discharged the following ministries while He was here on earth:

A. SALVATION: He is the Saviour. It was said of Him,

> *"And you shall call his name Jesus for he will save his people from their sins"* (Matthew 1:21).

The Lord's ministry of salvation is being continued by His Spirit and His Body.

B. BAPTISM INTO THE HOLY SPIRIT: He is the Baptizer into the Holy Spirit. John the Baptist said,

> *"I baptize you with water for repentance but he who is coming after me is mighter than I, whose sandals I am not worthy to carry. He will baptize you with the Holy Spirit and with fire"* (Matthew 3:11).

The Lord continues to baptize people into the Holy Spirit today either directly or through the laying on of the hands of the church.

C. TEACHING: He is the Master Teacher. The Bible says,

> *"And he opened his mouth and taught them saying..." (Matthew 5:1-2).*

> *"And he began to teach beside the sea" (Mark 4:1).*

The Lord continues His teaching ministry today through His Spirit (the Holy Spirit) and His Body (the Church).

D. HEALING: He is the Healer.

> *"For he had healed many, so that all who had diseases pressed upon him to touch him" (Mark 3:10).*

He continues His healing ministry today through His Spirit and His Body.

E. DELIVERANCE: He is the Deliverer. The Bible says,

> *"And immediately there was in their synagogue a man with an unclean spirit; and he cried out, "What have you to do with us Jesus of Nazareth? Have you come to destroy us? I know who you are, the Holy One of God," But Jesus rebuked him saying, "Be silent and come out of him," And the unclean spirit convulsing him and crying with a loud voice, came out of him" (Mark 1:23-26).*

THE DELIVERANCE MINISTRY OF THE LORD JESUS

Throughout most of the earthly ministry of the Lord Jesus, He was always casting out demons. The deliverance ministry of the Lord was prophesied. The prophet Isaiah had prophesied about Jesus saying of Him,

> *"The Spirit of the Lord God is upon me, because the Lord has anointed me to bring good tidings to the afflicted, he has sent me to bind up the broken-hearted, to proclaim liberty to the captives, and the opening of the prisons to those who are bound, to proclaim the year of the Lord's favour..." (Isaiah 61:1-2).*

During His earthly ministry, the Lord Jesus fulfilled that prophecy. One day, while in the synagogue in Nazareth, He opened the Word of God and read,

> *"The spirit of the Lord is upon me, because he has anointed me to preach the good news to the poor, he has sent me to proclaim release to the captives and recovering of sight to the blind, to set at liberty those who are oppressed, to proclaim the acceptable year of the Lord" (Luke 4:18-19).*

The Bible adds that

> *"He closed the book and gave it back to the attendant, and sat down, and the eyes of all in the synagogue were fixed on him. And he began to say to them, "Today this scripture has been fulfilled in your hearing" (Luke 4:20-21).*

The apostle John said,

DELIVERANCE FROM DEMONS

> "The reason the Son of God appeared was to destroy the works of the devil" (1 John 3:8).

Demons are part of the works of the devil and wherever Jesus encountered them, He delivered those who were in bondage to them.

GENERAL DELIVERANCE BY THE LORD JESUS

The Bible says,

> "And he went about all Galilee, teaching in their synagogues and preaching the gospel of the kingdom and healing every disease and every infirmity among the people. So his fame spread through all Syria, and they brought him all the sick, those afflicted with various diseases and pains, demoniacs, epileptics and paralytics and he healed them. And great crowds followed him from Galilee and the Decapolis and Jerusalem and Judea and from beyond the Jordan" (Matthew 4:23-25).

Again the Bible says,

> "That evening, at sundown, they brought to him all who were sick or possessed with demons. And the whole city was gathered together about the door. And he healed many who were sick and cast out many demons; and he would not permit the demons to speak because they knew him" (Mark 1:32-34).

SPECIFIC DELIVERANCE BY THE LORD JESUS.

1. When 3.000 to 6.000 demons inhabited one man:

THE MINISTRY OF JESUS TO DEMON - ATTACKED PEOPLE

"They came to the other side of the sea, to the country of the Gerasenes. And when he had come out of the boat, there met him out of the tombs a man with an unclean spirit, who lived among the tombs; and no one could bind him any more, even with a chain; for he had often been bound with fetters and chains, but the chains he wrenched apart and the fetters he broke in pieces; and no one had the strength to subdue him. Night and day among the tombs and on the mountain he was always crying out, and bruising himself with stones. And when he saw Jesus from afar he ran and worshiped him, and crying out with a loud voice, "What have you to do with me, Son of the Most High God? I adjure you by God, do not torment me." For he had said to him, "Come out of the man, you unclean spirit." And Jesus asked him, "What is your name?" He replied, "My name is legion, for we are many." And he begged him eagerly not to send them out of the country. Now a great herd of swine was feeding there on the hillside, and they begged him, "Send us to the swine, let us enter them." So he gave them leave. And the unclean spirits came out, and entered the swine; and the herd, numbering about two thousand, rushed down the steep bank into the sea, and were drowned in the sea.

The herdsmen fled and told it in the city and in the country. And people came to see what it was that had happened. And they came to Jesus, and saw the demoniac sitting there, clothed and in his right mind, the man who had the legion; and they were afraid. And those who had seen it told what had happened to the demoniac and to the swine. And they began to beg Jesus to depart from their neighbourhood. And as he was getting into the boat, the man who had been possessed with demons begged him that he might be with him. But he refused, and said to him, "Go home to your friends, and tell them how much the Lord had done for you, and how he has had mercy on you." And he went away and began to proclaim in the Decapolis

DELIVERANCE FROM DEMONS

how much Jesus had done for him; and all men marveled" (Mark 5:1-20).

This man apparently had an unclean spirit but indeed there were legions of demons in him. A legion was a military unit of 3,000 to 6,000 soldiers. The demons said that they were legion meaning that they were probably 3,000 - 6,000 of them. Can you imagine one man with 3,000 to 6,000 demons? It is awful, but it shows us what the possibilities are. One man can have up to 6,000 demons! If they are to be cast out one after another and if the process is slow as it sometimes is, then it can take weeks or months. I read of the deliverance of one person that took seven months to be completed. This man might initially have had one demon and then he co-operated with that demon and so others came in until he was "filled" with them. The demon spoke through the man. Sometimes, they spoke as one evil spirit and at other times they spoke as many demons. He talked of his name, but said that they were many.

These demons caused him to live among the tombs and in the mountains. They gave him such extraordinary power that he could not be chained. They caused him to bruise himself and to cry out.

When Jesus asked them to go out, they resisted. They acknowledged who He was and asked not to be disturbed. The man came and bowed down to Jesus and worshipped Him. When they knew that they had to leave, they negotiated with Jesus. They begged not to be sent out of the country. They begged to be sent into the swine. Jesus granted them their request. They entered the herd and it went and drowned. The man was totally restored and wanted to follow Jesus but the Lord sent him to his people where he filled ten cities (decapolis) with the message of the redeeming power of the Lord.

I believe that there are many people in the city of Yaounde like the demoniac whose deliverance is described here. I think of one in particular. At the initial stages, he wore clean clothes but moved about talking alone. Then his clothes became dirtier and dirtier. Later on, he went about with rags, and as time went on, he began to move about almost naked, to carry dirty things, to eat from dust bins, to rub himself with dung, to burn himself with fire until he died. The outward condition might have reflected the number of demons in him. Possibly he started with having one and later on, ended with thousands. Some possessed people end up stark mad and later on die.

The purpose of demons in taking hold of a man's mind and rendering him mad is to prevent him from thinking about the Gospel and repenting. Their purpose in killing him is to ensure that he never gets delivered and repents. When demons kill a demoniac, they have won the battle for ever.

Jesus accepted the plea of the demons to enter into the swine. The man became whole immediately he was delivered! No further prayer was necessary. The Lord spoke to all the demons at once. He did not cast them out one after the other. He cast them all out in one go. Today, we often cast demons out one after the other but we should bear in mind that the Lord did not do it that way. However, the ultimate thing is that the demons should be cast out. If there is limited authority that results in their being cast out one after the other, it is better than nothing. We must, nevertheless, aim at the day when, by God's grace, we will minister at the same level that Jesus did. All who are involved in the deliverance ministry should labour with the Lord to grow in that ministry.

2. Deliverance at a Distance:

> *"And he entered a house and would not have anyone know it; yet he could not be hid. But immediately a woman, whose little daughter was possessed by an unclean spirit, heard of him, and came and fell down at his feet. Now the woman was a Greek, a Syropheonician by birth. And he said to her, "Let the children first be fed, for it is not right to take the children's bread and throw it to dogs." But she answered him, "Yet even the dogs under the table eat the children's crumbs." And he said to her "For this saying you may go your way; the demon has left your daughter." And she went home, and found the child lying in bed, and the demon gone" (Mark 7:24-30).*

This woman came to seek the deliverance of her daughter. Jesus tested her faith and her faith stood the test. The daughter was not there but the Lord caused her to the delivered. With her faith, the mother plugged in on Jesus and the miracle took place when Jesus decided that it should.

I am beginning to learn the dimensions and the possibilities of the ministry of deliverance at a distance. In the near future, I plan to set aside one night a week in the Clinic for Spiritual Diseases for deliverance at a distance. If the Lord can deliver people who are present and the demons are commanded to leave in His name, then the same Lord can be trusted to deliver people who are separated by distance from the human being administering the deliverance. Deliverance is a matter of spiritual power and authority. These two elements need know no limitation by distance.

3. Deliverance from a special kind of demon:

THE MINISTRY OF JESUS TO DEMON - ATTACKED PEOPLE

"And when they came to the disciples, they saw a great crowd about them, and the scribes arguing with them. And immediately, all the crowd when they saw him, were greatly amazed, and ran to him and greeted him. And he asked them, "What are you discussing with them?" And one of the crowd answered him, "Teacher, I brought my son to you, for he has a dumb spirit; and whenever it seizes him, it dashes him down, and he foams and grinds his teeth and becomes rigid; and I asked your disciples to cast it out, and they were not able." And he answered them, "O faithless generation, how long am I to be with you? How long ought I to bear with you? Bring him to me. And they brought the boy to him; and when the spirit saw him, immediately it convulsed the boy, and he fell on the ground and rolled about, foaming at the mouth. And Jesus asked the father, "How long has he had this?' And he said, "From childhood. And it has often cast him into the fire and into the water, to destroy him; but if you can do anything, have pity on us and help us." And Jesus said to him, "If you can! All things are possible to him who believes." Immediately the father of the child cried out, and said, "I believe; help my unbelief!" And when Jesus saw that a crowd came running together, he rebuked the unclean spirit, saying to it, You dumb and deaf spirit, I command you, come out of him, and never enter him again." And after crying out and convulsing him terribly it came out and the boy was like a corpse, so that most of them said, "He is dead." But Jesus took him by the hand and lifted him up, and he arose. And when he had entered the house, his disciples asked him privately, "Why could we not cast it out?" And he said to them, "This kind cannot be driven out by anything but prayer and fasting" (Mark 9:14-29).

There are many important lessons about the deliverance ministry to be learnt from this ministry, that we shall comment fairly exhaustively on it.

a. The manifestation of the demons: That demon manifested itself as follows:

- dumbness
- deafness

These two manifestations were constantly there.

- dashing down
- foaming
- grinding of teeth
- becoming rigid
- convulsion
- rolling on the ground

These manifestations were only visible when the demon seized the body. They were occasional manifestations.

b. The Lord was not there when the man brought his son. His disciples failed to deliver him. The same disciples had carried out other deliverances in the past, but this time they failed. The deliverance of people who have demons is not something that a person can say that because he delivered someone before, he will necessarily deliver the next. Presumption is folly. Each case must be taken on its own. We shall look at the requirements for the deliverance ministry later on.

Suffice it to say that the Lord rebuked the disciples for lack of faith. Later on, He showed clearly that even if they had faith, that alone would have been insufficient. It was a special kind of demon that could only be cast out by prayer and fasting.

Demons are not all the same. They are in ranks, and the demands for deliverance from the different ranks are different;

- There are demons that will run away when they see any believer.
- There are some that will leave at the command of any believer.
- There are others that will leave at the commands of consecrated believer.
- Some will leave only if the consecrated believer has faith.
- Others will leave if the consecrated believer with faith prays and fasts.
- There are yet others that will leave only if the one ministering has the gift of working miracles and in addition, fasts and prays

c. The demands of the faith of the parents before deliverance could be ministered.

This boy was possessed by the demon. His whole personality was under the demon's control. The Lord could not demand faith from him but he demanded faith from the father. He said something like this, to the man; "Your son's deliverance does not depend on me. I am willing to deliver him. However, it will only be possible if you have faith. Do you have faith?" the man replied that he had faith which was not perfect and asked Jesus to help his imperfect faith.

When deliverance is being ministered to a totally possessed person, no contribution of faith can be expected from him. His relatives who bring him must believe . The one ministering must also have faith. His faith is primordial.

DELIVERANCE FROM DEMONS

When deliverance is being ministered to someone whose condition is such that he can have faith in the Lord Jesus for deliverance, he must exercise that faith or the demon would not leave. If the person would not exercise faith, the faith of the minister, however strong, will fail. We can sum it up like this:

condition of man needing deliverance	Requirement of his relatives	Requirement of him	Requirement of the minister of deliverance
Totally under demonic power	Faith in Jesus	None	Faith in Jesus
Partially under demonic power	None	Faith in Jesus	Faith in Jesus

I want to add that the relatives or the person who is being delivered must have some faith in the minister of deliverance.

There is no possibility of ignoring the human instrument. If a person believes that God will use this human instrument for deliverance, he is often prepared to exercise faith in the Lord and then the deliverance is possible. When he doubts if God will use that particular person, then rarely does anything happen. If someone says, "I have brought this person to you for deliverance but if you fail to deliver him I will go to the other person whose deliverance ministry is more outstanding. "It would be better that you do not attempt to minister to him. It will not work. Deliverance is not a matter of trying from here to there. Unless a man come to the end of himself, he cannot receive deliverance. If he has other possibilities he should be encouraged to go straight to those ones, after which, he will have nowhere else to turn to. As we shall see later, the human instrument is very important.

d. The power to cause demons to manifest themselves. When the spirit saw Jesus, immediately it convulsed the boy and he fell on the ground and rolled about, foaming at the mouth. Apparently those manifestation were not seen when only the disciples were there with the man and his son. People who walk close to the Lord, are filled with the Holy Spirit and his power, will cause demons to manifest themselves and his power, will cause demons to manifest themselves when normally they would not. Demons may be present in a manifest themselves under the ministry of a certain minister but when another person appears they will react. If a person is compromising with sin in one form or the other; His presence is unlikely to cause demons to manifest themselves as you minister, something is probably wrong with your relationship with Jesus. A thief in darkness will not react violently if the light of a small candle is brought in, but if a big, bright light is brought in, he will react violently, either in an attempt to escape, or in an attempt to destroy the light or the one who brought it in. There are people who hold that there are not demons in our day. Such people walk so far away from Jesus that their presence cannot cause demons to manifest themselves. Because they walk so far away from him, they ascribe all demonic manifestations to psychological disorders needing psychiatric treatment. Before I was baptized into the Holy Spirit, I never saw any demons manifest themselves in situations where I preached the gospel. I eased my conscience by saying that people were being induced psychologically. I know better now. In the

DELIVERANCE FROM DEMONS

Church in Yaounde, at the beginning, we used to confuse manifestations of demons with manifestation of the Holy Spirit now, we know better. There are always some demonic manifestations when the baptism into the Holy Spirit is being ministered to people. Is it not understandable that where the power of the Holy Spirit is being manifested in Glorious power, demons that did not react before should then react?

e. The demons often cast the boy into the fire and into the water to distroy him. That is their Goal to destroy people before they have come to repentance.

f. When the Lord commanded the demon to go, it did not go at once. It cried out, then convulsed the boy terribly and then left.

g. The boy looked like a corpse after he was delivered. I remember once in Western Buganda, we cast out a demon of insanity from a young man he was very noisy and agitated before we moved in to minister to him. We laid hands on him and prayed for him, commanding the demon to leave. After sometime, we took off our hands and the young man collapsed. He looked like a corpse and was in that condition for about one hour. The mother had a very worried look. She came to me and asked me what was happening. I had peace in my mind that all was well and told her so. Later on, he woke up, asked for food, ate and was normal and the nest day, returned to the advanced teachers college, where he was a student. Some people have felt thirsty immediately after deliverance and asked for something to drink. Others have asked for food. Others have been filed with thanksgiving and praise. One thing is certain, when deliverance is complete, there will be some manifestation of it in the visible.

h. Jesus asked the demon never to enter the boy again. This would indicate that that was necessary for the boy to remain delivered. I recommend that all ministers of deliverance should ask the demons that are cast out never to enter into the person again. I did not know this before and I found that some people who were delivered had demons in them again. Before, I thought that we had made mistakes about the deliverance the first time. Now I know that they can come back, and therefore, I command them never to come back into that again.

THE LORD JESUS AND DEMONIC DISEASES

By demonic diseases we mean diseases that are caused solely by demons. The diseases are manifestations of demons. Below are some instances of Jesus healing demonic diseases by deliverance.

1) The demon of Epilepsy:

The Bible says,

> *"And when they came to the crowd, a man came up to him and kneeling before him said, "Lord, have mercy on my son for he is an epileptic and he suffers terribly; for often, he falls into the fire and often into water..." And Jesus rebuked him, and the demon came out of him, and the boy was cured instantly" (Matthew 17:14-18).*

2)

> *"teacher, I brought my son to you for he has a dumb spirit... and wherever it seizes him, it dashes him down, and he foams and grinds his teeth and becomes rigid... It had often cast him into the fire and water, to destroy him... you dumb and deaf spirit I*

command you, come out of him, and never enter him again..."
(Mark 9:17-29).

This demon threw the boy into the fire and water just as the preceding one but the other was a spirit of epilepsy while this one was a spirit of dumbness and deafness. One must not superficially name a demon because it manifests itself like another demon that he had cast out before. Each situation must be faced with an open mind and dependence on the Lord for revelation. When the deaf and dumb spirits were cast out the boy was healed forthwith.

3) The Demon of Dumbness

The Bible says,

> "As they were going away, behold, a dumb demoniac was brought to him. And when the demon had been cast out, the dumb man spoke" (Matthew 9:32-33).

4) The demon of Dumbness and Blindness:

> "Then a blind and dumb demoniac was brought to him, and he healed him, so that the dumb man spoke and saw" (Matthew 12:22).

5) The Spirit of Infirmity:

> "Now he was teaching in one of the synagogues on the Sabbath. And there was a woman who had had a spirit of infirmity for eighteen years; she was bent over and could not fully straighten herself. And when Jesus saw her, he called her and said to her, "woman, you are free from your infirmity. And he laid his hands upon her and immediately she was made straight and she praised God... Then the Lord

answered him, "You hypocrites! Does not each one of you on the Sabbath untie his ox or his as from the manger, and lead it away to water it? And out not this woman, a daughter of Abraham whom Satan bound for eighteen year be loosed from this bond on the Sabbath day?" As he said this, all his adversaries were put to shame; and all the people rejoiced to at all the glorious things that were done by him" (Luke 13:10-17).

It would seem to me that of many people who stretch themselves, some are bound by demons.

In this deliverance, Jesus first spoke worlds of comfort to her, then laid his hands on her and immediately she was made straight. It is obvious that the demon of infirmity departed with the laying on of the Lord's hands. She had been bound for eighteen year. I wonder how many doctors she had seen! If the Lord had not delivered her, she would possibly have died in that condition.

We can make the following conclusions from the ministry of the Lord to people with demonic diseases.

A) There are diseases that are organic in nature. Such will yield to medical treatment or healing in the name of the Lord Jesus. There are others that result from the presence of demons. For such, medical treatment will not help anything. Spiritual healing will not avail anything. There is only one answer and it is deliverance in the name of Jesus and that will be followed by instant healing. Those diseases that are organic will not respond to the deliverance ministry.

B) The Lord Jesus did not confuse healing and deliverance. He clearly distinguished between the two and handled each case as the need demanded. The Bible says,

DELIVERANCE FROM DEMONS

"And he healed many who were sick with various, diseases AND CAST OUT many demons" (Mark 1:34)

"That evening they brought to him many who are possessed with demons; and he cast out the spirits with a word, and healed all who were sick" (Matthew 8:16)

How is one distinguish between the sickness that is of organic nature and that one which is demonic manifestation? The answer is in the gift of discernment of spirits. Believers who are involved in the deliverance ministry should covet this gift, lay hold on God and receive it. There is also the capacity for discernment that those who have walked for a considerable length of time with the Lord in close fellowship, knowing the word and obeying it, have. I suggest that if there is a disease that would not respond to:

- medical treatment,
- The laying on of hands for healing in the name of Jesus
- The anointing with oil in the name of Jesus
- The anointing with oil and the prayer of faith by the elders of the local Assembly,

then its origin is most likely demonic and the person should be delivered.

C) Finally, there is the possibility that healing and deliverance can take place simultaneously. The Bible says of the Lord Jesus,

"Now when the sun was setting, all who had any that were sick with various diseases brought them to him, and he laid his hands on

everyone of them and healed them. And demons also came out of many crying" you are the Son of God' but he rebuked them, and would not allow them to speak, because they knew that he was the Christ " (Luke 4:40-41).

Here we do not notice any specific ministry of deliverance. It would seem that while the sick were being healed, the presence of the Lord caused demons to come out crying.

My prayer and desire for all who minister deliverance is that we will so walk in intimacy and purity before the Lord, so that his power will continuously be upon us,. The result will be that some demons will go away from the people they inhabit just by noticing our presence.

4

THE MINISTRY OF BELIEVERS TO DEMON-ATTACKED PEOPLE

A) HOW DO DEMONS GET INTO HUMAN BEINGS ?

Before we consider the deliverance ministry of believers, let us, first of all, consider how demons get into human beings we know that the devil is on the move

> *"going to and fro on the earth and walking up and down on it"* (*Job 1:7*)

we also know that "the devil prowls around like a roaring lion, seeking someone to devour" (1Peter 5:8) Demons like their master, may be expected to be going to and fro and walking up and down on earth, seeking whom they may devour. This means that any persons or any areas that are not protected, are open to them. If they find no opening. They will stay outside and attack from outside. If they find and opening. They will enter into the person and try to destroy from inside. They will use the smallest opportunities that are opened to them. Such opportunities can be as follows:

DELIVERANCE FROM DEMONS

1. By living continuously under conditions of:

- strains,
- distress,
- anxiety,
- shock,
- anger, to name a few.

Children who live under such condition are clearly exposed to evil spirits. Take for example, the spirit of inferiority complex is often the lot of illegitimate children or children from broken homes or children who are orphans with no one to take real care of them. It may start with self-doubt that persists, then the demon of inferiority comes in, having seen an opening. Children who live in home where the father and the mother are often quarrelling and disagreeing with each other, live in fear and insecurity and are therefore open to demons. This inferiority may manifest itself as pride, self-will, stubbornness, but it is essentially self-doubt and an opening to demons. Parents who are constantly screaming and shouting at their children open them up to demons in their constant state of fear.

2) By the practice of magic in one form or the other; by living with people who practice magical arts or by living in the vicinity where it is practised, and by belonging to secret societies, and the like. It is close to impossible to practise magic and not be inhabited by a demon or demons. Magic being something which is fundamentally of Satan, grips those who practise it and hands them over to the devil. It is as if the one who practises magic is saying to demons, "Look, I am here. Why don't you come and dwell in me?" Demons will not spare such opportunities that are more or less freely

THE MINISTRY OF BELIEVERS TO DEMON-ATTACKED PEOPLE

given. It is for this reason that when people who have been in such things believe, they should be delivered. It is folly to take for granted that when Jesus came into the person's life, the demons just left without being asked to do so.

3) Idolatry has to do directly with demons. The Bible says, "They stirred him to jealousy with strange gods; with abominable practices they provoked him to anger. They sacrificed to demons which were gods, to gods they had never known, to gods that had come in of late, whom your fathers had never dreaded (Deuteronomy 32:12-17)

> *"They served their idols, which became a snare to them. They sacrificed their sons and their daughters to demons" (Psalm 106:36-37)*

> *"I imply that what the pagans sacrifice they offer to demons and not to God. I do not want you to be partners with demons" (1Corinthians 10:20).*

Idolatry is not only practised by pagans. We know that Babylon represents false Christianity where some things or people such as:

- Statues,
- Images,
- "saints"
- "holy Mary"

have been allowed to take the place of the Lord Jesus. Of her the Bible says,

> *"It has become a dwelling place of demons, a haunt of every foul spirit, a haunt of every foul and hateful bird" (Revelation 18:2)*

4) By being baptised into Satan in one form or the other.

5) By being handed to the devil in exchange for:

- power,
- wealth,
- success,
- and the like.

In 1975, I was invited to cast a demon out of a child of about nine yeas old. The parents wanted to trick me. They tied things from sorcerers in various parts of the child's body and then covered her with a white garment hoping that I would not know what was under. I laid my hands on the child and commanded the demon to leave. The demon spoke aloud saying that the child was his because she been voluntary given to him by the parents. I called the parents and talked to them. The y had consistently taken her to sorcerers and made sacrifices on her behalf. The demon had therefore come into her and considered her his property. I asked the parents to repent before I would deliver the child. The mother said that they should repent but the father said that they had done nothing to be repented of. I quietly left them with their child, for there was no ground on which I could by-pass the parents and deliver the child.

B) WHO CAN MINISTER DELIVERANCE?

1. The Lord Jesus said,

> "and there signs will accompany those who believe: in my name they will cast out demons; they will speak in new tongues; they will pick up serpents, and if they drink any deadly thing, it will not hurt

THE MINISTRY OF BELIEVERS TO DEMON-ATTACKED PEOPLE

them; they will lay their hands on the sick and they will recover" (Mark 16:17-18).

Every believer has the potential, by virtue of his position in Christ, to minister deliverance. However, not all believers can cast out all demons. It is a matter of warfare and the Bible says, "for though we live in the world, we are not carrying on a worldly war, for the weapons of our warfare are not worldly but have divine power to destroy strongholds. We destroy arguments and every proud obstacle to the knowledge of God, and take every thought captive to obey Christ, being ready to punish every disobedience when your obedience is complete." (2 Corinthians 10:3-6).

Deliverance means that a person is able to punish demons for their disobedience. Those whose obedience to the Lord is say 25% may inflict punishment on demons up to 25%. Those whose obedience to the Lord is say 50%, may inflict punishment on demons up to 50% those whose obedience to the Lord is 90% may inflict punishment on demons up to 90%. Those whose obedience to the Lord in 100% may inflict punishment on demons up to 100%

Demons can see through a person. They know those who are obedient and those whose obedience is partial. They know whom they must obey and they know whom they can disobey. They know that if they attempt to disobey those who are totally obedient, they would face the full force of God's power and be ruined. They also know that they can disobey the disobedient ones without suffering any consequences. Demons spoke in Bible times to some people and said,

"Jesus I know, and Paul I know, but who are you?" (Acts 19:15).

Demons ask the disobedience either in part or in whole, "who are you?" they says to all such, "If you are prepared to disobey God, we too, are prepared to disobey you." The Lord expects that those who would go out in his name be people whose consecration to him is total; who are not disobeying him in any area of their lives. To such He gives unqualified authority over demons. He says to them as He said to the disciples of old,

> "and he called the twelve together and gave them power and authority over all demons and to cure diseases, and he sent them out to peach the kingdom and to heal" (Luke 9:1-2)

> "Behold I have given you authority to tread upon serpents and scorpions, and over all the power of the enemy; and nothing shall hurt you" (Luke 10:19)

If you are living in sin in any area of your life, you are throwing away your mandate to minister deliverance. The extent to which a person can minister deliverance is determined by the power of the Lord that flows through him. The power of the Lord is available through:

- discipline,
- a knowledge of the word,
- a holy ad consecrated life,
- Spiritual gifts,
- prayer,
- Christlikeness in character.

All these ways through which spiritual power become available, are tied to obedience. The obedient will grow increasingly in spiritual power.

THE MINISTRY OF BELIEVERS TO DEMON-ATTACKED PEOPLE

2) Those who would minister deliverance must recognized the power (authority) that is vested on them in the name of Jesus and learn to use it I am not just talking of a theological or Biblical (Logos) knowledge of the power of the Lord Jesus. The knowledge that I am thinking about is that which comes by personal revelation of the authority that is in the name of the Lord Jesus, and personal revelation on how to use it. I am talking of the Rhema knowledge of the power of the Lord Jesus.

3) those who would minister deliverance must know the victory of Jesus on the cross. When Jesus when to the cross, He look the devil and his whole army with him and disarmed them. The Bible say:

"He disarmed the principalities and powers and made a public example of them, triumphing over them in him" (Colossians 2:15).

He has disarmed the demons. They can be cast out. The devil is the strong man of the house. The Lord conquered him on the cross and made deliverance possible. Because Satan was conquered, his army can be outed. The knowledge of the victory of Christ on the cross will enable you to stand firm and command demons to go, and insist that they go and they will go. In commanding them to go, you are not begging them. You are ordering them. When commanded to leave, they will look at you thoroughly to see if they can find any reason in you to stay. If they find none, they will go away.

4) He must be a man of prayer and fasting. As we have seen, there are some demons which will only be cast out by praying and fasting. How is one to distinguish this kind from the other ones? Is he to command them to come out in the name of Jesus and if they do not come out he will then know that that kind comes out only by fasting and praying and so organize a fast to prepare? That would be poor ministry. It would be ministry by trial and error. The best thing is that those who would minister deliverance should fast and pray regularly as a way of life so that this, coupled with unconditional obedience to the Lord all the time, will place them in a position where they are more than equal to any demon that they may encounter. At the time Jesus told the disciple of a demon which could only come out by praying and fasting, there is a sense in which the disciples could not cast out that particular demon. This is because they were not yet given to fasting, the bridegroom being still with them. Our situation now is different. The Lord is away. We are to fast and pray and cast out all kinds of demons.

5) He must forgive all who have wronged him. The power to deliver from demons is the power of the Lord Jesus. If the minister of deliverance is harbouring ill-feelings, he will block the power of the Lord for deliverance from flowing through him to other. The Lord said,

> *"For if you forgive men their trespasses, your heavenly father also will forgive you; but if you do not forgive men their trespasses,, neither will you heavenly father forgive your trespasses" (Matthew 6:14-15).*

I do not think that anyone of us does not need the daily forgiveness of God. (I personally need his forgiveness daily, hourly and every minute). Because we need his forgiveness, we must forgive other or else, we will be separated from him because of our trespasses. We insist that there must be an unhindered relationship with people (as far it depends on those who carry out deliverance) for the ministry to be

THE MINISTRY OF BELIEVERS TO DEMON-ATTACKED PEOPLE

successful. An unforgiving spirit indicates that the person is himself bound. How then can a prisoner set other free? He must set himself free and then he will be able to liberate the others.

C) REQUIREMENTS OF THE PERSON NEEDING DELIVERANCE

(in the case where he has a demon or demons but is not possessed).

The person with the demon or demons must do the following:

1. He must desire deliverance. A person may have a demon but may not want to be delivered. God will not force deliverance on such a person. He will allow his freedom of will to prevail.
2. He must be willing to admit that he has a demon, for example, if a person has a demon of gluttony but says, "I am not too bad. I over eat occasionally, that is all." He cannot be delivered. If he grows fat because of gluttony and then says, "well, I come from a family of fat people; I am not actually overweight, I will not have money for new clothes, and so on", he will not be delivered, for he is not willing to admit that he has a demon. To admit that one has a demon is humbling. Most people are too proud to humble themselves, admit that they have a demon and be delivered. God cannot bless the proud. He abases them.
3. He must be willing to submit to the ministry of deliverance; A person may say, "Well, I guess I have a demon but I am holier than everybody here. Who is

spiritual enough to deliver holy me? " He may say, "I think everybody here has a demon. I will wait until I find that special person to whom I can submit and be delivered." Such a person will remain in bondage. He is too proud. He resembles the prince of demons-Satan.

4. He must repent of all the known sins in his life, confess and forsake them. The bible says, *"he who commits sin is of the devil; for the devil has sinned from the beginning the reason the Son of God appeared was to destroy the work of the devil No one born of God commits sin, for God's nature abides in him, and he cannot sin because he is born of God. By this it may be seen who are the children of God and who are the children of the devil : whoever does not do right is not of God, nor he who does not love his brother "(1 John 3:8-10).* Sin is co-operation with the devil. Wherever there is sin the devil has legal grounds to stay. So, before a person can be delivered he must bring all the grounds that the devil could have for staying in him to an end. He must part radically with all the sin in his life.

5. He must put an end to all dealing with the supernatural realm of the devil. Demons probably got into him because of his contact with idols or sorcery in one form or the other. To be delivered, the person must publicly renounce all such things and terminating that have to do with the forbidden supernatural of those things, the deliverance is likely to fail, for the person has not yet gotten to the point where he wants the kingdom of Satan to be completely overthrown.

6. He must forgive all who have wronged him in any way. An unforgiving heart, bitterness, hatred, malice,

and so on, are the elements that hold the kingdom of the devil together. If these things are retained in any life, demons are most likely not going to obey the command to leave such a life. They will continue to stay and they should.

7. He must believe that deliverance is possible in the name of Jesus. Deliverance is not possible because of a powerful servant of God. It is not possible because of a powerful servant of God. It is not possible because of such prayer and fasting good as these things are. It is possible because Jesus conquered the devil on the cross, two thousand year ago and took away his authority and power. Without looking on to Jesus who is the deliverance, even the must powerful looking on to Jesus who is the deliverance, believing that Jesus will set me free now!"

8. He must call upon the name of Lord Jesus for deliverance. He must come to the end of himself and be willing to be delivered forthwith. If he can go on for another day, week, the person who is ready for deliverance is the one who says, "I am desperate. I must be delivered here and now! I submit now to deliverance, believing that Jesus will set me free now!"

D) THE ACT OF DELIVERANCE

If the one who is to minister deliverance and the one to receive the ministry of deliverance are both ready, they may then proceed in the following manner:

DELIVERANCE FROM DEMONS

1) The person to receive the deliverance should d pray asking the Lord to deliver him. (This is not necessary if the person is in a condition in which he cannot pray).

2) The one ministering the deliverance should command the demon or demons that are present to manifest themselves. Sometimes, at that command, the demon, the demon may manifested itself as follows:

- screaming,
- shouting,
- shaking,
- weeping,
- laughing,
- singing,
- choking,
- Knocking people over,
- convulsion,
- coughing,
- groaning,
- fainting,
- writhing,
- spitting,
- vomiting
- speaking in an unknown tongue,
- running away,
- talking a posture of prayer,
- tearing of clothes,
- undressing,

3) The manifestations are so varied that the minister should expect anything. There have been time when the demons have begun to manifest themselves without anyone asking for any manifestations. No one should br put off by those manifestations. Sometimes, no obvious manifestation are visible. That does not necessarily mean that no demon or demons are present. They may be trying to hide themselves Sometimes, manifestations only come with insistence.

The one ministering deliverance should command the demon to give its name. This has two-fold effect. First of all, it compels the demon to expose itself. When a demon has given its name, it will be more difficult for it to hide. Secondly, in giving its name, there is proof that the person who wants deliverance is prepare to own up, and expose the demon, since demons are creatures that prefer darkness and deception, naming them will help to weaken their authority.

The Lord took the information that demons gave to be true even through they were capable of lying. I suggest that the information that is given by demons, that is, the names, numbers, how long they have been in the person, should be believed without asking if the demon (or demons) is lying. Such a question is in a way useless, for if demons lied the first time, they can tell another lie and say that it is the truth.

If there is more than one person involved in the deliverance, there should be one person who leads the team and who does the talking to the demons. He will weigh what is being said and co-ordinate it and thereby decide how the deliverance is to proceed. It is unwise for a group of people to surround a demon-possessed man and one says one thing, another, another thing altogether. The kingdom of the Enemy is very organized and the demon can only utilise such disorder to maintain their stay in the person. Some of the names given by demons may sound very strange. They should not be rejected because they are strange. A demon that identified

DELIVERANCE FROM DEMONS

itself as the demon of Hitler was cast out in our country. Demons can take on many names and many forms. The Angels of the Lord sometimes take on the form of human beings. Demons which are the angels of Satan can do the same. I have often heard that people have met people who were dead and buried, in human form after their burial, and that sometimes these disappeared on recognition I did not believe this for many years. (I am generally not prone to believing). However, I now think that demons possibly take the forms of dead men and go about in them either to discredit them or for Virgin Mary. This can be nothing other than demons talking her form and be lost. In the word of God, when the rich man who was in hell asked that someone be sent to his brothers from the land of the dead, he was told that if someone went to earth from the land of the dead, the people will not believe either. Mary is in the grave. Demons are using her form or a form similar what she looked like). The painting are fanciful imaginations to deceive the children of the devil one so that they may worship her unto their damnation.

4) when a demon has given its name, it should be denounced by the one in whom it dwells. For example, it a demon of anger has been named, the person should speak to the demon saying, you demon of anger, I denounce you in the name of the Lord Jesus and command your illegal stay in me to come to and end now. There will be many occasion where such are orderly affair is impossible. It could be that the demon is very violent or that it is trying to strangle the person if that is so, then the deliverance has to proceed as the circumstances dictate. There is no formula.

5) The one ministering the deliverance must now command the demon to come out immediately. Sometimes, they linger and torment the person. On some other occasions, they will hide or withdraw their manifestations, giving the impression that they have left. Whatever the case may be, the one ministering the deliverance must press on until there is real deliverance should find out if there are so on. Sometimes, they do spit on the face of the minister of deliverance, doing everything to make him as uncomfortable as possible. At other times, the person vomits so much and the vomit has such an awful odour, just in a bid to resist being cast out. Sometimes, they undress the person and try to seduce the minister of deliverance. They will do everything to try and stay. When they do leave, it is obvious that they have left. The manifestations stop suddenly and the person's appearance changes.

It is often easy to distinguish when they speak from when the person who has the demon is speaking. It is not difficult after e few cases of deliverance to learn how to distinguish the two voices.

Sometimes, there is communication between two spirits in deliver different people in a room. Once we had a difficult time in delivering some people until we realized that the demons were communicating with each other and thereby reinforcing their stay. We broke the communication, in the name of Jesus, and soon the deliverance was accomplished. At other times, we found that a number of demons in one person were reinforcing each other and thereby making deliverance difficult. We used the name of the Lord Jesus to separate the deliverance from each other, bound each and cast it out and then the deliverance was effected. Casting out demons can be very tiring for both the person who has the demon and for the one who is ministering so that, sometimes, a break is necessary. This should not be considered as

DELIVERANCE FROM DEMONS

a mark of weakness. The important thing is that the deliverance should be resumed and completed. No minister of deliverance should be so busy that he has no time to terminate the deliverance that he started. There are people who are fundamentally disorganized and who are quick to start projects but they do not carry them through a finish. Anyone who starts sessions of deliverance and does not terminate them, dishonours God. If he allows his indiscipline to continue, he may find that the Lord will take away from him the power to effect the ministry of deliverance.

6) When the deliverance has been accomplish, the demons should be commanded not to return into the person.

7) After deliverance, the person should not really believe before. Now, he is certainly in a better condition. He should be helped to come to the Lord for salvation. When he has received the Saviour, he should be baptized into water at once and after that he should be led to Jesus, the one who baptized into the Holy Spirit so that he should be baptized into the Holy Spirit at once. The will give him a normal beginning of the Christian life.

The person should be taught to terminate radically with the past and that is the subject matter of the next chapter. We recognise and even inhabited by a demon or demon is because they did not terminate with the past in the way that they ought to have done started the life in Christ, to carefully read the next chapter and put it into practice.

Finally, it is good that deliverance is followed by a ministry of praised to the deliverer. This should include.

- Prayer of praise and thanksgiving
- Songs of praise and thanksgiving.

- Testimonies of praise and Thanksgiving.

I recommend that deliverance be carried out normally and regularly as part of the ministry of the local church just as the other ministries, such as:

- baptism into the Holy Spirit,
- evangelism
- teaching,
- healing...

I also suggest that deliverance should be carried out in teams. In one situation where I carried out deliverance all alone, I had such a hard time with the demoniac, who was so wild and fierce that by the time that the deliverance was completed, after a violent two hours, the young man collapsed under fatigue and I was very close to fainting. In fact, I stayed put on the floor for two hours. A team of people will also help in circumstances where the demons want to kill the person by strangling or any such thing. The Bible says,

> *Two are better than one, because they have a good reward for their toil. For if they fail, one will lift up his fellow; but woe to him is alone when he falls and has not another to lift him up" (Ecclesiastes 4:9)*

10). However, the team should be well organized. Each person must know his position before the Lord, before demons and in relationship to the other member of the team.

5

KEEPING FREE FROM DEMONS OR TERMINATING WITH THE PAST

"Therefor, if any one is in Christ, he is a new creation; the old has passed away, behold, the new has come" (2 Corinthians 5:17).

When a person receives the Lord Jesus as his Lord and Saviour, the Lord forgives him all sins and blots away all that stood against him i the heavenly record. However, for him to grow properly in the new life, he must deliberately co-operate with God by terminating with his past life.

1. TERMINATING WITH RELATIONSHIP WITH THE SUPERNATURAL

The supernatural realm is in two dimensions: the supernatural that relates to God who is the Father of our Lord and Saviour Jesus Christ and the supernatural which relates tot he devil and all his principalities and power. The supernatural dealing with God is to be encouraged and the supernatural dealing with the devil is to be terminated with.

DELIVERANCE FROM DEMONS

Young converts, before you receive the Lord, you might have had the following contacts with forbidden supernatural practices:

1. the practice of magic,
2. contact with sorcerers in one form or the other.
3. contact with the dead and the worship of ancestor,
4. attempts to foretell the future through astrology, e.g. horoscope, palmistry, mediums, fortune tellers and the like.
5. contact with mystical secret societies of foreign origin like the Rosicrucian orders (ARMOC), Free Masons, Yoga Transcendental Meditation, Lodges, and so on.
6. contact with mystical secret societies of local origin like:

- Ogboni society, Famla, Nyamkwe, Obassinjom, Ngondo, and so on.
- talismans ans amulets for personal protection.
- charms and all that is used to influence others, e.g love portions used to seduce and maintain the love of others.
- brain prills and all that are used to acquire intelligence or examination successes.
- the use of magical powers for success in football and other games.

You must break with the at once. The life of God in you, through the Lord Jesus, is entirely oppose to those supernatural activities of the devil, so that you cannot continue in them as a child of God. In the past, while you were a child of the devil, you could continue in the practice that originated with your father the devil. Now, You have changed parentage: you have changed kingdom. You must learn all that belong the kingdom which you have abandoned.

God is opposed to those practices. He says, "You shall no practice augury or witchcraft... You shall not make any cutting in your flesh on account of the dead or tattoo any marks upon you: I am the Lord" (Leviticus 19:26-28).

> "Do not turn to mediums or wizards; do not seek them our, to be defiled by them: I am the Lord your God" (Leviticus 19:31).

> "There shall not be found among you anyone who burns his sons and his daughters as an offering, anyone who practices divination, a soothsayer or and augur, or a sorcerer, or a charmer, or a medium or a wizard, or a necromancer. For whosoever does these things is an abomination to the Lord. (Deuteronomy 18:10-12).

God punishes all who have dealings with such things. His Word says,

> "You shall not permit a sorcerer to live" (Exodus 22:18).

> "If a person turns to mediums and wizards, playing the harlot after them, I will set my face against that person and will cut him off from among his people" (Leviticus 20:27).

> "But as for ... sorcerer... their lot shall be in the lake that burns with fire and sulphur, which is the second death" (Revelation 21:8).

You are to break with them not because they are impotent. No. Sometimes they have power. Sometimes their revelations are true and their predictions correct. Sometimes their knowledge is true. The problem is not whether or not they are correct. The crucial question is, "What is their origin?" Whom do they serve? Do the offer only temporary help or do they offer eternal help?"

All these practices use the power of the devil. The devil is their originator. He gives them a beginning and sustain them . For that reason, all that come from them is to be rejected even if it appears helpful. In Philippi, there was a slave girl with a spirit of divination that brought a owner great gain by soothsaying. The spirit even recognised Paul and Silas and spoke what was true about them say:

> "The men are servants of the Most High God, who proclaim to you the way of salvation" (Acts 16:17).

What was being said was true but the source was from the devil. Paul could have allowed it in the hope that her pronouncement would help the people to believe him and his message. He could have said, "It is the truth. It will help irrespective of the source." Of course he knew that the source being the devil could not help God. Nothing from the devil can help God. All healing by sorcerers, witch doctors, and so on, are from the devil's kingdom. They can never help the kingdom of God. You must never just ask, "Is this goo or bad? Is it profitable or unprofitable?" You must ask, "Is this of God or of Satan?" Satan may offer things that appear good. They are all to be rejected. God may offer things that may appear bad. They are all to be received with thanksgiving. So Paul turned and said to the spirit,

> "I charge you in the name of Jesus Christ to come out of her." And it came out that very hour" (Acts 16:18).

Paul perhaps knew that such an action would bring them trouble, nevertheless, he did it. He was not out to compromise. True servants of the Lord proclaim and practise the whole truth at any cost. He did not say, "Le me leave the girl alone so that my ministry may not have complications." No! He cast out the spirit and got imprisonment as a well-earned "thank you". The only way to further the Kingdom of God is to denounce all the work of the devil. Please, put an end to all of them.

a) The Ephesian example.

The Bible says about the Ephesian believers,

> *"Many also of those who were now believers came again, confessing and divulging their practices. And the number of those who practice magic acts brought their books together and burned them in the sight of all, and they counted the value of them and found that it came to fifty thousand pieces of silver. So the word of God grew mightily" (Act 19:18-20).*

We can learn the following from these believers:

- They, did not hide deeds of darkness in which thy were involved prior to their conversion to Christ. They exposed them and confessed them.
- They destroyed everything that had to do with their sinful past, expensive as they were.
- These things were destroyed (burned) publicly and not thrown away privately.
- This action resulted in spiritual growth for the work of the Lord.

You, too, must not hide any magical activities which once involved. Expose them and expose them. Bring all these things to the Assembly of God's children so that they should be destroyed regardless of what they have cost you. In this way, you will continue to the growth of the Gospel. You have no choice about this.

b) Idolatry

In the first and second commandment, God says to man,

> *"You have no other God besides me. You shall not make for yourself a graven image, or any likeness of anything that is in heaven above, or that is in the earth beneath, or that is in the water under the earth; you shall not bow them to them or serve them"* (Exodus 20:3-5).

Idolatry includes having anything, persons, systems, philosophy on the throne of the heart, above, beside or nest to God. God must have the first place in an absolute sense. It also includes the making of any image of God or man or anything to represents God. It includes the bowing to objects, the making and keeping of picture of "Jesus" and the like. All this is idiolatry.

If you set up yourself in that position in life where you are prepared to do what you think or like or want instead of what God wants, you should know that you are an idolater. Anyone who deliberately sin, that is, he deliberately does what he knows that God does not want, has raised himself to the place of final authority and is unquestionably an idolater.

If your job, ambition, education, wife (or husband), children, parents government, girlfriend or (boyfriend) or any other thing, takes the first place in your life, you are an idolater. To know if you are worshipping anything can be tested very easily by the following test:

- Has God asked me not to have this thing? If you still keep it after the Lord has asked you to get rid of it, then you are worshipping it.
- Does this thing hinder my walk with God in any way? If it hinders your walk with God are you still keep it, you are worshipping it.
- Am I prepare to let it go any moment that the Lord ask me to let it go? If you are hesitant or unwilling, you are worshipping it.

All that you are worshipping are idols. You must put an end to them! Images and statues of God or Jesus or Mary or any other "saint"; relics from "saints" being kept for their magical healing power, other wooden, stone, metallic or any form of image, are to be destroyed. You cannot bow to an image of Jesus and also bow to Jesus. All who bow to images or make , keep, distribute and sell them, are enemies of the Lord Jesus.

The supposed pictures of Jesus or any other personality in the Bible are the devil's lies. No pictures were taken of anyone in the Bible. The pictures that are said to be the pictures of Jesus are the products of minds that are enmity with God.

What of saints as intermediaries? What of saints praying for us? What of holy Mary praying for us? These are all the devil's lies. There is one God and only one intermediary between God and man - Jesus. All other intermediaries are abominations to God and to people who know Him. The Bibles,

"For there is one God and there is one mediator between God and me, the man Christ Jesus, who gave himself as a ransom for all, the testimony to which was born at the proper time" (1 Timothy 2:5-6).

"How much more shall the blood of Christ, who through the eternal spirit offer himself without blemish to God, purify your conscience from dead works to serve the living God. Therefore he (Jesus Christ) is the mediator of a new covenant so that those are called may received the promised eternal inheritance, since a death has occurred which redeems them from the transgressions under thee first commandment" (Hebrews 9:14-15).

All ceremonies that are carried out even in the name of the Lord Jesus, by men who worship religious idols and was and have other intermediary apart from Jesus are dead works. When they repent from dead works and come to the Lord Jesus and to Him alone, they will be redeemed by Him. You cannot be redeemed by Jesus and be redeemed by the holy Mary.

C) Getting rid of idols.

All idols must be gotten rid of so that the idol worshipper can turn to the Lord in spirit and truth worship Him as he deserves to be worshipped. The Bible says,

"but the hours is coming and now is, when the true worshippers will worship the Father in spirit and in truth. God is spirit, and those who worship him must worship him in spirit and in truth" (John 4:23-24)

God is spirit and not a statue, not an image. He is to be worship in spirit and in truth and not with rosaries and lies.

How do we get rid of idols ? Let us learn from the example of Gideon.

Gideon was called by the Lord. He knew God. God had planned to use him, but before God could use him for other purposes, God had to use him to pull down idols, the bible says,

> "that night the Lord said to him, take your father's bull, the second bull of seven years old, and to him, take your father's bull, the second bull of seven year old, and pull down the altar of ball which your father has and cut down the asherah that is beside it; build an altar to the Lord your God on the top of the stronghold here, with stones in due order. The take the second bull, and offer it as a offering with the wood of the Asherah which you shall cut down. So Gideon took ten men of his servants and did as the Lord had told him" (Judges 6:25-27)

How did the people react? They wanted to kill him (Judges 6:30). How did God react to it? The bible says,

> But the spirit of the Lord took possession of Gideon" (Judges 6:34).

You, too, must do the same. Break down and destroy all idols. Then offer a sacrifice of your life to the Lord. He will received it and in return he will let His Spirit possess you. Will you be Gideon today? What is God asking you to part with? What is God asking you to break down? Will you obey?

d) Rejecting the influence of satanic powers.

You may have been brought up in an atmosphere where the devil was worshipped in one way or the other? One member or are involved in witchcraft or satanic practices in one way or the other. By their action you are passively involved. You may even been dedicated to the devil or been baptized into Satan. A sorcerer or astrologer, may have been consulted on your behalf. You are, therefore, not free.

To get free from these entanglement, I suggest that you confess your own sins in this area also the sins of your parents or relatives then actively, by calling upon the name of the Lord Jesus, break all the bonds strong or weak that bind you to your family as far as these supernatural involvements are concerned and take your stand out of that family, and into the family of God. Tell the devil that from that moment, his power over you as a result of such activities is broken for even. Tell him that by your act now of breaking with your parent's supernatural involvement and taking cover under the blood of Jesus, you have no part in all the activities that your parents may carry out in your name from now on and for ever. By that act of breaking with the past, you stand totally free in the Lord Jesus.

DO NOT FEAR

You may be afraid to throw away all the rings charms, and so on, and to break down all the idols that you know you should break, for fear that the devil will react. Indeed he will surely react, but nevertheless, do not fear. The Lord Jesus who lives in you is stronger than the devil. The Bible says,

> "Little children, you are of God, and have overcome them; for he who is in you is greater than he who is in the World" (1 John 4:4).

The Lord Jesus said: "Behold I have given you authority to tread upon serpents and scorpions, and over all the power of hell is impotent against you as you stand fully protected in Christ.

May be what you fear is physical death or suffering that will result from your destruction of Idols that must be destroyed. Do not fear. The Lord Jesus said,

> *"and do not fear those who kill the body but cannot kill the soul; rather fear him who can destroy both the soul and body in hell"* (Matthew 10:28)

Also bear in mind that even as far as your physical life is concerned, no harm can come to you without the permission of your heavenly Father. All that He permits will ultimately result in a blessing for you. Pilate said to Jesus: "Do you not know that I have power to release you, and power to crucify you?" Jesus answered him, "you would have no power over me unless it had been given you from above; therefore he who delivered me to you has the greater sin (John 19:11).

You, too, should rest assured that no one have power over you unless he were allowed from heaven and what God allows will turn out for your ultimate good.

Look at Jesus. Have eternity in view. Fear God and do what he wants. Say to yourself, "The Lord is for me, who can be against me and succeed?"

2 TERMINATING WITH PAST SEXUAL RELATIONSHIPS.

Before you knew the Lord you may have had boyfriends (Or girlfriends), men or women in your life who were not your legal partners. You may have been keeping a woman as a concubine. You may have had a steady sex partner or you had several sex partners. You may have been masturbating or been involved in homosexual practices in one form or the other. You may have been reading dirty novels or involved in questionable petting. You may have been engaged to or hoping to be engaged to an unbeliever. You may have continued to have sexual relationships with the father or mother of your illegitimate child or children. You may have had special delight in pornography you are to stop all such practices. You are to break all such relationships and you are to break them at once.

The Bible says,

> "Do you not know that the unrighteous will not inherit the kingdom of God? Do not be deceived: neither fornicators, nor idolators, nor adulterers , nor sexual partners, nor thieves, nor the greedy, nor drunkards, nor robbers will inherit the kingdom of God. And such were some of you, but you were sanctified, you were justified in the name of the Lord Jesus Christ and in the spirit of our God" (1Corinthians 6:9-11)

Again the word of God says,

> "Do not be mismated with unbelievers. For what partnership have righteousness and iniquity ? Or what fellowship has light with darkness ? What accord has Christ with Belial ? Or what has a believer in common with an unbeliever? What agreement has the temple of God with idols? For we are the temple of the living God, as God said, I will live in them and move among them, and I will be their God and they shall be my people. Therefore come out from them, and be separated from them, says the Lord, and touch nothing unclean, then I will welcome you, and I will be a father to you, and

you shall be my sons and daughters, says the Lord almighty" (2 Corinthians 6:14-18).

You as a believer cannot marry an unbeliever ! The unbeliever belongs to the devil. You belong to God. The devil cannot be married to God. There is an eternal divorce between the two. You may be engaged to an unbeliever but let me tell you that you that your conversion has brought that engagement to an end. You are the temple of God How can you continue in an engagement with someone who is the temple of the devil? You are clean. The unbeliever is unclean. The Bible says,

"Touch not the unclean thing."

You may be haunted by past sexual relationships. The devil may bring to your memory past sexual relationships in order to bring you back to the things that you have abandoned. Reject these suggestions. Stand firm on your authority in the name of the Lord Jesus and reject all the ties that link you to your sinful past. Break the power of the sexual sins in the name of Jesus and you shall find that you are delivered completely. If there is an unbeliever in your life who does not want to leave you, pray in this fashion, "In the name of the Lord Jesus, I command Mrs/Mr/miss X to get out of my life now so that I may be free always.

As you take that stand in prayer and refuse all co-operation with the devil, you will experience victory and deliverance. God bless you.

One thing that will help you to break any ties with undesirable people is to turn anything that they gave you as part of the price for your body. For example, if a man gave you money, household goods, musical equipment, or other things as part of the price for using you, then when you have received the Lord Jesus, you must return his property. If you do not do so, those things will remind you of the wicked past and then the devil will continue to torment you. It is costly but your total freedom in Christ is far more important than all that you may part with. Another reason why you must return all proceeds from sinful relationships is that unless you do so. You have no testimony before that person. He will not take your conversion seriously until you have returned the price that he paid for your body! If you received goods which are now lost or have become old from use, if you received goods which are now lost or have become old from us, use, you should calculate the equivalent and pay that person in cash. This is the way of the new life. Finally, you should stop seeing that person. Introduce him to another believer who should then try to reach him for Christ. If you attempt to reach him yourself you may find yourself in fresh entanglements.

3. TERMINATING WITH PROFESSIONS THAT DISHONOUR CHRIST

If before you conversion you worked for a tobacco company you must stop working for that company. It is not God's will that people should destroy themselves by smoking. Your body is the temple of the Holy Spirit (1 Corinthians 6:19). You must not destroy God's temple with smoking and the accompanying diseases. If you do, God will destroy you (1 Corinthains 6:16-17) Tobacco is bad for you and for all the creatures of God. You must contribute in any way towards its production or use. So, stop smoking at once. Stop giving cigarettes to people. Stop selling cigarettes and stop working

KEEPING FREE FROM DEMONS OR TERMINATING WITH THE PAST

for cigarette production company. Ask God for a new occupation that honours him.

The same applies to alcohol. The Bible says, "Wine is a mocker, strong drink a brawler; and whoever is led astray by it is not wise" (Proverbs 20:1). Stop drinking alcohol. Stop serving alcohol. Stop helping in the production of alcohol in any way. The Bible says that no helping in the production of alcohol in any way. The Bible says that no drunkard will inherit the kingdom of God. (1 Corinthians 6:10) No one is born a drunkard. You may give a man the first glass of drink that will lead him on the way of ruin as a drunkard and finally to hell. Dare you do that? So, do not drink alcohol. Do not go to bars and drinking houses. They are the devil's workshops for destroying health, life, family and the nation.

Do not go to night clubs. They are places frequented by empty men and women who have lost their sense of direction in life. They are also the devil's workshops. If you are working in a night club, please terminate with it. That is not the place for you.

Do not go to worldly films. Imagine all the bloodshed, immorality and crime that is displayed on the screen. Is that what you want to fill your mind with? Certainly not. So, do not go there. Do not help anyone to go there. Do not work there.

As you terminate with these unfruitful works of darkness, you should trust the Lord to help you to find the job that he has in tore for you, where you can truly serve him. He will supply all your needs. The Bible says:

> *"have no anxiety about anything, but in everything, but in everything by prayer and supplication with thanksgiving let your request*

be made known to God And the peace of God which passe all understanding, will keep your heart and your minds in Christ Jesus" (Philippians 4 :6-7)

Furthermore, the word of God says:

"And my God will supply every need of yours according to his riches in glory in Christ Jesus" (Philippians 4:19).

4. TERMINATING WITH UNHEALTHY FAMILY TIES

You belonged to an earthly family before conversion. At conversion you were born into the family of God. Your first loyalty must now be to the Lord and his family. This does not mean that you stop being helpful to your family members. It simply means that if the demands of your husband, wife, children, parents, and others, conflict with the demands of the Lord Jesus, You will go ahead at once and obey the Lord Jesus. There must be no question about this at all. It is Jesus first. The Bible says,

"Now great multitudes accompanied him and he turned and said to them, "If any one comes to me and does not hate his own father and mother and wife and children and brother and sisters, yes and even his own life, he cannot be my disciple" (Luke 14:25-26).

Jesus said:

"Do not think that I have come to bring peace on earth; I have not come to bring peace, but a sword. For I have come, to set a man against his father, and a daughter against her mother-in law; and a man's foes will be those of his own household. He who loves father and mother more than me is not worthy of me; and he who loves

father and daughter more than me is not worthy of me; and he who love son and daughter more than me is not worthy of me" (Matthew 10:34-37).

Love your family but let your loyalty be to the Lord Jesus and the household of God.

The proverb says: "Like father, like son, "We tend to carry with us family character traits. Some of these are assets and others are liabilities. Some family traits which children take over from their parents and which are liabilities include:

- laziness,
- indiscipline,
- gluttony,
- restlessness,
- temper and
- untidiness.

You should break with these character flaws that you took over from your parents or the people in whose environment you were brought up. Claim the power of the Lord Jesus and be delivered from these.

There are also hereditary traits e.g. baldness, early grey hair and sickle cell anaemia, and so on, which are inherited from parents without any personal choice whatsoever. From parent without any personal choice whatsoever. One should break with these in the name of Jesus. The Bible says:

> *"But he was wounded for our transgressions, he was bruised for our iniquities, upon him was the chastisement that made us whole and with his stripes we are healed"* (Isaiah 53:5).

When the Lord went to the cross, he took all our sicknesses and diseases, as well as all our infirmities with him and nailed them to his cross. He took sickle cell anaemia genes as well as all other undesirable genes with Him to the cross. We can be free from all these. They are part of our inheritance. We should also claim our healing from all diseases and deformities in the name of Jesus. Perfect health and perfect form are yours in the Lord Jesus.

5. TERMINATING WITH CHRISTLESS SOCIAL TRADITIONS

There are social traditions that blind people and enslave them. Some of these include: expensive birth celebrations, death celebrations and the offering of libations at parties. These are purely worldly traditions that are unhelpful. You are not to indulge in them. Keep yourself pure for the Lord. Be free to serve him and to serve Him alone.

PRINCIPLES OF CONDUCT

To help you to decide whether or not to carry out a certain practice, ask yourself the following questions:

1. Who is the author of this? Is it God or Satan? If God is the author then there is the possibility that you can do it.
2. Who will this action glorify? Is it God or Satan or self? Do not do it if it will glorify Satan or self.
3. Will it help me to grow in Christ or will it retard me? Only do what will help you to grow.
4. Will it put me in conditions where I may be tempted. If So, keep away from it.

5. Will it help others to see Christ in me? If not, do not do it, for you are ambassador for Christ.
6. Will others do the same thing and perhaps fall into sin even though you can do it without falling into sin? If the activity is likely to cause a young believer to fall, then out of love for him, do not do it.
7. Will it lead to a habit from which I may not easily set myself free? If so, do not do it.
8. Is it the right time for it? Something may be right when done at a particular time but wrong at a different time. There is a time for everything. (Ecclesiastes 3:1-8).

Finally, the Holy Spirit will guide you. Look up to him. The Lord Jesus said: "When the Spirit of truth comes, he will guide you into all the truth" (John 16:13).

BACK MATTER

THANK YOU

For Reading This Book

If you have any question and/or need help, do not hesitate to contact us through **ztfbooks@cmfionline.org**. If the book has blessed you, then we would also be grateful if you leave a positive review at your favourite retailer.

ZTF BOOKS, through Christian Publishing House (CPH) offers a wide selection of best-selling Christian books (in print, eBook & audiobook formats) on a broad range of topics, including marriage & family, sexuality, practical spiritual warfare, Christian service, Christian leadership, and many more. Visit us at **ztfbooks.com** to learn more about our latest releases and special offers. And thank you for being a ZTF BOOK reader.

We invite you to connect with more from the author through social media (**cmfionline**) and/or ministry website (**ztfministry.org**), where we offer both on-ground and remote training courses (all year round) from basic to university level at the *University of Prayer and Fasting (WUPF)* and the *School of Knowing and Serving God (SKSG)*. You are highly welcome to enrol at your soonest convenience. A FREE online Bible Course is also available.

Finally, we would like to recommend to you another suitable book in this direction - *The Way Of Spiritual Warfare*

In this book, Z.T. Fomum exhorts the Church to support the gospel enterprise through an active and dynamic prayer life. The nature of the enemy, his army, his weapons and his strategies are well explained in this book.

He speaks substantively of the authority with which God has endowed the church. This authority is a heritage that Jesus Christ acquired for each believer by his death on the cross, where Satan was vanquished and disgraced forever. Jesus, by His death on the cross, did not conquer only the devil but also every illness, infirmity and sickness.

In this book, the author demonstrates that all human beings are engaged in fierce spiritual conflict. All unbelievers are in Satan's camp actively or passively engaged in the conflict. No one in this world is neutral.

Believers are expected to be fully committed in Jesus' camp. Their main weapons are obedience and prayer. This is a book of indisputable depth, with an edifying and revealing prophetic dimension.

VERY IMPORTANT!!!

If you have not yet received Jesus as your Lord and Saviour, I encourage you to receive Him. Here are some steps to help you,

ADMIT that you are a sinner by nature and by practice and that on your own you are without hope. Tell God you have personally sinned against Him in your thoughts, words and deeds. Confess your sins to Him, one after another in a sincere prayer. Do not leave out any sins that you can remember. Truly turn from your sinful ways and abandon them. If you stole, steal no more. If you have been committing adultery or fornication, stop it. God will not forgive you if you have no desire to stop sinning in all areas of your life, but if you are sincere, He will give you the power to stop sinning.

BELIEVE that Jesus Christ, who is God's Son, is the only Way, the only Truth and the only Life. Jesus said,

VERY IMPORTANT!!!

> "I am the way, the truth and the life; no one comes to the Father, but by me" (John 14:6).

The Bible says,

> "For there is one God, and there is one mediator between God and men, the man Christ Jesus, who gave himself as a ransom for all" (1 Timothy 2:5-6).

> "And there is salvation in no one else (apart from Jesus), for there is no other name under heaven given among men by which we must be saved" (Acts 4:12).

> But to all who received him, who believed in his name, he gave power to become children of God..." (John 1:12).

BUT,

CONSIDER the cost of following Him. Jesus said that all who follow Him must deny themselves, and this includes selfish financial, social and other interests. He also wants His followers to take up their crosses and follow Him. Are you prepared to abandon your own interests daily for those of Christ? Are you prepared to be led in a new direction by Him? Are you prepared to suffer for Him and die for Him if need be? Jesus will have nothing to do with half-hearted people. His demands are total. He will only receive and forgive those who are prepared to follow Him AT ANY COST. Think about it and count the cost. If you are prepared to follow Him, come what may, then there is something to do.

INVITE Jesus to come into your heart and life. He says,

VERY IMPORTANT!!!

"Behold I stand at the door and knock. If anyone hears my voice and opens the door (to his heart and life), I will come in to him and eat with him, and he with me " (Revelation 3:20).

Why don't you pray a prayer like the following one or one of your own construction as the Holy Spirit leads?

> "Lord Jesus, I am a wretched, lost sinner who has sinned in thought, word and deed. Forgive all my sins and cleanse me. Receive me, Saviour and transform me into a child of God. Come into my heart now and give me eternal life right now. I will follow you at all costs, trusting the Holy Spirit to give me all the power I need."

When you pray this prayer sincerely, Jesus answers at once and justifies you before God and makes you His child.

*Please write to us (**ztfbooks@cmfionline.org**) and I will pray for you and help you as you go on with Jesus Christ.*

ABOUT THE AUTHOR

Professor Zacharias Tanee Fomum was born in the flesh on 20th June 1945 and became born again on 13th June 1956. On 1st October 1966, He consecrated his life to the Lord Jesus and to His service, and was filled with the Holy Spirit on 24th October 1970. He was taken to be with the Lord on 14th March, 2009.

Pr Fomum was admitted to a first class in the Bachelor of Science degree, graduating as a prize winning student from Fourah Bay College in the University of Sierra Leone in October 1969. At the age of 28, he was awarded a Ph.D. in Organic Chemistry by the University of Makerere, Kampala in Uganda. In October 2005, he was awarded a Doctor of Science (D.Sc) by the University of Durham, Great Britain. This higher doctorate was in recognition of his distinct contributions to scientific knowledge through research. As a Professor of Organic Chemistry in the University of Yaoundé 1, Cameroon, Professor Fomum supervised or co-supervised more than 100 Master's Degree and Doctoral Degree theses and co-authored over 160 scientific articles in leading international journals. He considered Jesus Christ the Lord of Science ("For by Him all things were created..." – Colossians 1:16), and scientific research an act of obedience to God's command to "subdue the earth" (Genesis 1:28). He therefore made the Lord Jesus the Director of his research laboratory while he took the place of deputy director, and attributed his outstanding success as a scientist to Jesus' revelational leadership.

In more than 40 years of Christian ministry, Pr Fomum travelled extensively, preaching the Gospel, planting churches and training spiritual leaders. He made more than:

- 700 missionary journeys within Cameroon, which ranged from one day to three weeks in duration.
- 500 missionary journeys to more than 70 different nations in all the six continents. These ranged from two days to six weeks in duration.

By the time of his going to be with the Lord in 2009, he had preached in over 1000 localities in Cameroon, sent over 200 national missionaries into many localities in Cameroon and planted over 1300 churches in the various administrative provinces of Cameroon. At his base in Yaoundé, he planted and built a mega-church with his co-workers which grew to a steady membership of about 12,000. Pr Fomum was the founding team-leader of Christian Missionary Fellowship International (CMFI); an evangelism, soul-winning, disciple making, Church-planting and missionary-sending movement with more than 200 international missionaries and thousands of churches in 65 nations spread across Africa, Europe, the Americas, Asia and Oceania. In the course of their ministry, Pr Fomum and his team witnessed more than 10,000 recorded healing miracles performed by God in answer to prayer in the name of Jesus Christ. These miracles include instant healings of headaches, cancers, HIV/AIDS, blindness, deafness, dumbness, paralysis, madness, and new teeth and organs received.

Pr Fomum read the entire Bible more than 60 times, read more than 1350 books on the Christian faith and authored over 150 books to advance the Gospel of Jesus Christ. 5 million copies of these books are in circulation in 12 languages as well as 16 million gospel tracts in 17 languages.

Pr Fomum was a man who sought God. He spent between 15 minutes and six hours daily alone with God in what he called Daily Dynamic Encounters with God (DDEWG). During these DDEWG he read God's Word, meditated on it, listened to God's voice, heard God speak to him, recorded what God was saying to him and prayed it through. He thus had over 18,000 DDEWG. He also had over 60 periods of withdrawing to seek God alone for periods that ranged from 3 to 21 days (which he termed Retreats for Spiritual Progress). The time he spent seeking God slowly transformed him into a man who hungered, thirsted and panted after God. His unceasing heart cry was: "Oh, that I would have more of God!"

Pr Fomum was a man of prayer and a leading teacher on prayer in many churches and conferences around the world. He considered prayer to be the most important work that can be done for God and for man. He was a man of faith who believed that God answers prayer. He kept a record of his prayer requests and had over 50, 000 recorded answers to prayer in his prayer books. He carried out over 100 Prayer Walks of between five and forty-seven kilometres in towns and cities around the world. He and his team carried out over 57 Prayer Crusades (periods of forty days and nights during which at least eight hours are invested into prayer each day). They also carried out over 80 Prayer Sieges (times of near non-stop praying that ranges from 24 hours to 120 hours). He authored the Prayer Power Series, a 13-volume set of books on various aspects of prayer; Supplication, Fasting, Intercession and Spiritual Warfare. He started prayer chains, prayer rooms, prayer houses, national and continental prayer movements in Cameroon and other nations. He worked with leaders of local churches in India to disciple and train more than 2 million believers.

Pr Fomum also considered fasting as one of the weapons of Christian Spiritual Warfare. He carried out over 250 fasts ranging from three days to forty days, drinking only water or water supplemented with soluble vitamins. Called by the Lord to a distinct ministry of intercession, he pioneered fasting and prayer movements and led in battles against principalities and powers obstructing the progress of the Gospel and God's global purposes. He was enabled to carry out 3 supra – long fasts of between 52 and 70 days in his final years.

Pr Fomum chose a lifestyle of simplicity and "self- imposed poverty" in order to invest more funds into the critical work of evangelism, soul winning, church-planting and the building up of believers. Knowing the importance of money and its role in the battle to reach those without Christ with the glorious Gospel, he and his wife grew to investing 92.5% of their earned income from all sources (salaries, allowances, royalties and cash gifts) into the Gospel. They invested with the hope that, as they grew in the knowledge and the love of the Lord, and the perishing souls of people, they would one day invest 99% of their income into the Gospel.

He was married to Prisca Zei Fomum and they had seven children who are all involved in the work of the Gospel, some serving as missionaries. Prisca is a national and international minister, specializing in the winning and discipling of children to Jesus Christ. She also communicates and imparts the vision of ministry to children with a view to raising and building up ministers to them.

The Professor owed all that he was and all that God had done through him, to the unmerited favour and blessing of God and to his worldwide army of friends and co-workers. He considered himself nothing without them and the blessing of God; and would have amounted to nothing but for them. All praise and glory to Jesus Christ!

- facebook.com/cmfionline
- x.com/cmfionline
- instagram.com/cmfionline
- pinterest.com/cmfionline
- youtube.com/cmfionline

RECOMMENDED BOOKS

https://ztfbooks.com

THE CHRISTIAN WAY

1. The Way Of Life
2. The Way Of Obedience
3. The Way Of Discipleship
4. The Way Of Sanctification
5. The Way Of Christian Character
6. The Way Of Spiritual Power
7. The Way Of Christian Service
8. The Way Of Spiritual Warfare
9. The Way Of Suffering For Christ
10. The Way Of Victorious Praying
11. The Way Of Overcomers
12. The Way Of Spiritual Encouragement
13. The Way Of Loving The Lord

THE PRAYER POWER SERIES

1. The Way Of Victorious Praying
2. The Ministry Of Fasting
3. The Art Of Intercession
4. The Practice Of Intercession
5. Praying With Power
6. Practical Spiritual Warfare Through Prayer
7. Moving God Through Prayer
8. The Ministry Of Praise And Thanksgiving
9. Waiting On The Lord In Prayer

10. The Ministry Of Supplication
11. Life-Changing Thoughts On Prayer (Vol. 1)
12. The Centrality of Prayer
13. Life-Changing Thoughts On Prayer (Vol. 2)
14. Prayer and Spiritual Intimacy
15. Life-Changing Thoughts on Prayer (Vol. 3)
16. The Art of Worship
17. Life-Changing Thoughts on Prayer (Vol. 4)
18. Life-Changing Thoughts on Prayer (Vol. 5)
19. Learning to Importune in Prayer
20. Prayer And A Walk With God
21. From His Prayer files
22. Prayer and Holiness
23. Practical Helps in Fasting Long Fasts
24. Life-Changing Thoughts on Fasting (Vol 1)
25. Life-Changing Thoughts on Fasting (Vol 2)
26. Pray Without Ceasing
27. Pray or Perish

PRACTICAL HELPS FOR OVERCOMERS

1. Discipleship at any cost
2. The Use Of Time
3. Retreats For Spiritual Progress
4. Personal Spiritual Revival
5. Daily Dynamic Encounters With God
6. The School Of Truth
7. How To Succeed In The Christian Life
8. The Christian And Money
9. Deliverance From The Sin Of Laziness
10. The Art Of Working Hard
11. Knowing God - The Greatest Need Of The Hour

12. Restitution - An Important Message For The Overcomers
13. Revelation: A Must
14. The Overcomer As A Servant Of Man
15. True Repentance
16. You Can Receive A Pure Heart Today
17. You Can Lead Someone To The Lord Jesus Today
18. You Can Receive The Baptism Into The Holy Spirit Now
19. The Dignity Of Manual Labour
20. You Have A Talent!
21. The Making Of Disciples
22. The Secret Of Spiritual Fruitfulness
23. Are You Still A Disciple Of The Lord Jesus?
24. Who Is Truly a Disciple of The Lord Jesus?

LEADING GOD'S PEOPLE

1. Vision, Burden, Action
2. Knowing The God Of Unparalleled Goodness
3. Brokenness: The Secret Of Spiritual Overflow
4. The Secret Of Spiritual Rest
5. Spiritual Aggressiveness
6. The Character And The Personality of The Leader
7. Leading A Local Church
8. The Leader And His God
9. Revolutionary Thoughts On Spiritual Leadership
10. Leading God's People
11. Laws Of Spiritual Leadership
12. Laws Of Spiritual Success, Volume 1
13. The Shepherd And The Flock
14. Basic Christian Leadership

15. A Missionary life and a missionary heart
16. Spiritual Nobility
17. Spiritual Leadership in the Pattern of David
18. The Heart Surgery for the Potential Minister of the Gospel
19. Prerequisites For Spiritual Ministry
20. Power For Service
21. In The Crucible For Service
22. Qualifications For Serving in The Gospel
23. You, Your Team, And Your Ministry
24. Church Planting Strategies
25. Critical Ingredients for Successful Spiritual Leadership
26. Knowing God And Walking With Him
27. The Power of a Man's All

GOD, SEX AND YOU

1. Enjoying The Premarital Life
2. Enjoying The Choice Of Your Marriage Partner
3. Enjoying The Married Life
4. Divorce And Remarriage
5. A Successful Marriage; The Husband's Making
6. A Successful Marriage; The Wife's Making
7. Life-changing Thoughts On Marriage

OFF-SERIES

1. Inner Healing
2. No Failure Needs To Be Final
3. Facing Life's Problems Victoriously
4. A Word To The Students

5. Blessings and Curses
6. Spiritual Fragrance (Volume 1)
7. Roots And Destinies
8. Walking With God (Vol. 1)
9. God Centredness
10. Victorious Dispositions
11. The Processes Of Faith
12. Knowing and Serving God (Volume 2)
13. Esther
14. The Church: Rights And Responsibilities of The Believer
15. Children in God's Eternal Purposes
16. Relationship and Intimacy With God
17. Victorious Proclamations

THE SPIRIT-FILLED LIFE

1. In The Power of Another
2. The Spirit-Filled Life

GOD, MONEY AND YOU

1. The Christian And Money
2. God, Money, And You
3. Giving to God
4. Treasures in Heaven

PRACTICAL HELPS IN SANCTIFICATION

1. Deliverance From Sin
2. The Way Of Sanctification

3. Sanctified And Consecrated For Spiritual Ministry
4. The Sower, The Seed, And The Hearts Of Men
5. Freedom From The Sin Of Adultery And Fornication
6. The Sin Before You May Lead To Immediate Death: Do Not Commit It!
7. Be Filled With The Holy Spirit
8. The Power Of The Holy Spirit In The Winning Of The Lost
9. Deliverance from the Sin of Gluttony
10. A Vessel of Honour
11. The Believer's Conscience
12. Practical Dying to Self and the Spirit-filled Life
13. Issues of The Heart
14. Rebellion
15. The Cross in Personal Relationships

MAKING SPIRITUAL PROGRESS

1. The Ministers And The Ministry of The New Covenant
2. The Cross In The Life And Ministry Of The Believer
3. Making Spiritual Progress, Volume 1
4. Making Spiritual Progress, Volume 2
5. Making Spiritual Progress, Volume 3
6. Making Spiritual Progress, Volume 4
7. Moving on With The Lord Jesus Christ
8. The Narrow Way (Volume 1)
9. Making Spiritual Progress (Volumes 1-4)

EVANGELISM

1. 36 Reasons For Winning The Lost To Christ
2. Soul Winning, Volume 1
3. Soul Winning, Volume 2
4. The Winning of The Lost as Life's Supreme Task
5. Salvation And Soul-Winning
6. Soul Winning And The Making Of Disciples
7. <u>Victorious Soul-Winning</u>

GOD LOVES YOU

1. God's Love And Forgiveness
2. The Way Of Life
3. Come Back Home My Son; I Still Love You
4. Celebrity A Mask
5. Encounter The Saviour
6. Meet The Liberator
7. Jesus is The Answer

JESUS STILL HEALS TODAY

1. Jesus Loves You And Wants To Heal You
2. Come And See; Jesus Has Not Changed!
3. Jesus Saves And Heals Today
4. Miracles, Healings, and Deliverances

WOMEN OF THE GLORY

1. The Secluded Worshipper: Prophetess Anna
2. Unending Intimacy: Mary of Bethany

3. Winning Love: Mary Magdalene

ZTF COMPLETE WORKS

1. The School of Soul Winners and Soul Winning
2. The Complete Works of Z.T.F on Holiness (Volume 1)
3. The Complete Works of Z.T.F on Basic Christian Doctrine
4. The Complete Works of Z.T.F on Marriage (Volume 1)
5. The Complete Works of Z.T.F on The Gospel Message (Volume 1)
6. The Complete Works of Z.T.F on Prayer (Volume 1)
7. The Complete Works of Z.T.F on Prayer (Volume 2)
8. The Complete Works of Z.T.F on Prayer (Volume 3)
9. The Complete Works of Z.T.F on Prayer (Volume 4)
10. The Complete Works of Z.T.F on Prayer (Volume 5)
11. The Complete Works of Z.T.F on Leadership (Volume 1)
12. The Complete Works of Z.T.F on Leadership (Volume 2)
13. The Complete Works of Z.T.F on Leadership (Volume 3)
14. The Complete Works of Z.T. F on Leadership (Vol 4)

SPECIAL SERIES

1. A Broken Vessel
2. The Joy of Begging to Belong to the Lord Jesus Christ: A Testimony
3. Separation from the common

4. My Separation from the Common unto God and World Conquest

AUTO-BIOGRAPHICAL SERIES

1. From His Lips: About The Author
2. From His Lips: About His Co-Workers
3. From His Lips: Back From His Missions
4. From His Lips: About Our Ministry
5. From His Lips: On Our Vision
6. From His Lips: The work is the worker
7. From His Lips: The Battles He Fought
8. From His Lips: The Authority And Power of His Life
9. From His Lips: The Influences That Moulded Him: People And Books

THE OVERTHROW OF PRINCIPALITIES

1. Deliverance From Demons
2. The Prophecy Of The Overthrow Of The Satanic Prince Of Cameroon
3. The Prophecy of the Overthrow of The Satanic Prince of Yaounde
4. The Prophecy of the Overthrow of The Satanic Prince of Douala
5. The overthrow of principalities and powers
6. From His Lips: The Battles He Fought

OTHER BOOKS

1. The Missionary as a Son

2. What Our Ministry is
3. Conserver la Moisson
4. Disciples of Jesus Christ to Make Disciples For Jesus Christ
5. The House Church in God's Eternal Purposes
6. Christian Maturation
7. Heroes of the Kingdom
8. Spiritual Leadership in the Pattern of Gideon
9. The School of Evangelism
10. A Good Minister of Jesus Christ
11. Building a Spiritual Nation: The Foundation
12. Building a Spiritual Nation: Spiritual Statesmanship
13. Watching in Prayer
14. The Character of the Christian Worker
15. Church and Mission
16. Strategic Missionary Work
17. The Power of Brokenness

PRAISE, PRAYER, AND FASTING CRUSADES

1. The Chronicles of Our Ministry [PFC2017]
2. Preparing to Encounter God [PFC2019]
3. The Making of Disciples: The Master's Way [PFC2020]
4. Removing Obstacles Through Prayer and Fasting [PFC2021]
5. Building a Spiritual Nation: Learning From Biblical Models [PFC2022]

OUR DISTRIBUTORS

These books can be obtained in French and English Language from any of the following distribution outlets:

EDITIONS DU LIVRE CHRETIEN (ELC)

- **Location:** Paris, France
- **Email:** editionlivrechretien@gmail.com
- **Phone:** +33 6 98 00 90 47

INTERNET

- **Location:** on all major online retailers
- **Email**: ztfbooks@cmfionline.org
- **Phone**: +47 454 12 804
- **Website**: ztfbooks.com

OUR DISTRIBUTORS

CPH YAOUNDE

- **Location:** Yaounde, Cameroon
- **Email:** editionsztf@gmail.com
- **Phone:** +237 74756559

ZTF LITERATURE AND MEDIA HOUSE

- **Location:** Lagos, Nigeria
- **Email:** zlmh@ztfministry.org
- **Phone:** +2348152163063

CPH BURUNDI

- **Location:** Bujumbura, Burundi
- **Email:** cph-burundi@ztfministry.org
- **Phone:** +257 79 97 72 75

CPH UGANDA

- **Location:** Kampala, Uganda
- **Email:** cph-uganda@ztfministry.org
- **Phone:** +256 785 619613

CPH SOUTH AFRICA

- **Location:** Johannesburg, RSA
- **Email:** tantohtantoh@yahoo.com
- **Phone**: +27 83 744 5682

Printed in Great Britain
by Amazon